Praise for Jonas V. Bilenas

"I found *The Power of PROC FORMAT* very easy to follow and would definitely recommend that beginning and intermediate SAS users buy this book and have it among their manuals to fully acquire the power of SAS and to assist themselves in becoming power users as well as efficient developers."

Charles Patridge
Senior Consultant, Deloitte Consulting

Online Samples — Examples from This Book at Your Fingertips

Companion Web Sites

You can access the example programs for this book by linking to its Companion Web site: **support.sas.com/companionsites.** Select the book title to display its Companion Web site, then select **Example Code** to display the SAS programs that are included in the book.

Anonymous FTP

You can use anonymous FTP to download ASCII files and binary files (SAS data libraries in transport format). To use anonymous FTP, connect to FTP.SAS.COM and enter the following responses as you are prompted:

Name (ftp.sas.com:user-id): anonymous
Password: <your e-mail address>

When you are logged on, download one or more example program files to your local directory:

get /pub/publications/A##### <your-local-filename>
(for ASCII files) or

get /pub/publications/B##### <your-local-filename>
(for binary files)

where ##### is the 5-digit order number that appears on the front cover of the book. If you need a list of all available example files, download the file **/pub/publications/index**.

SASDOC-L Listserv

Through the SASDOC-L listserv, you can download ASCII files of example programs from this book. By subscribing to SASDOC-L, you also receive notification when example programs from a new book become available.

To subscribe to SASDOC-L, send e-mail with a blank subject line to **LISTSERV@VM.SAS.COM.** The body of the message should be

SUBSCRIBE SASDOC-L <firstname lastname>

To download the file for a book, send this message to **SASDOC-L@VM.SAS.COM:**

get A##### examples sasdoc-l

where ##### is the 5-digit order number that appears on the front cover of the book.

Comments or Questions?

If you have comments or questions about this book, you may contact the author through SAS by

Mail: SAS Institute Inc.
          SAS Press
          Attn: <Author's name>
          SAS Campus Drive
          Cary, NC 27513

E-mail: saspress@sas.com

Fax: (919) 531-9439

Please include the title of the book in your correspondence.

See the last pages of this book for a complete list of books available through **SAS Press** or visit **support.sas.com/pubs.**

SAS Press

The Power of
PROC FORMAT

Jonas V. Bilenas

The Power to Know

The correct bibliographic citation for this manual is as follows: Bilenas, Jonas V. 2005. *The Power of PROC FORMAT.* Cary, NC: SAS Institute Inc.

The Power of PROC FORMAT

Copyright © 2005, SAS Institute Inc., Cary, NC, USA

ISBN 1-59047-573-9

1st printing, March 2005

SAS Publishing provides a complete selection of books and electronic products to help customers use SAS software to its fullest potential. For more information about our e-books, e-learning products, CDs, and hard-copy books, visit the SAS Publishing Web site at **support.sas.com/pubs** or call 1-800-727-3228.

Table of Contents

Preface vii
Acknowledgments ix
Using This Book xi

1 Introduction to SAS Informats and Formats 1

   1.1 Chapter Overview 2

   1.2 Using SAS Informats 2
      1.2.1 INPUT Statement 3
      1.2.2 INPUT Function 7
      1.2.3 INPUTN and INPUTC Functions 8
      1.2.4 ATTRIB and INFORMAT Statements 8

   1.3 Using SAS Formats 9
      1.3.1 FORMAT Statement in Procedures 10
      1.3.2 PUT Statement 11
      1.3.3 PUT Function 13
      1.3.4 PUTN and PUTC Functions 14
      1.3.5 BESTw. Format 14

   1.4 Additional Comments 17

2 Why Use PROC FORMAT? **19**

2.1 Chapter Overview..**20**

2.2 Table Lookups...**20**
    2.2.1 Binary Search Algorithm Used by SAS to Evaluate User-Defined Formats and Informats **22**

2.3 Data Sets Used in the Book **22**
    2.3.1 Adult Growth Hormone Deficiency Survery Data....................**23**
    2.3.2 Hypothetical Credit Score Data...**25**

3 VALUE and INVALUE Statements: Syntax and Examples **27**

3.1 Chapter Overview..**28**

3.2 Introductory Example **28**
    3.2.1 Using the IF-THEN/ELSE Statement **29**
    3.2.2 Using the VALUE Statement **30**

3.3 Internal SAS Character Informats and Impact on User-Defined Formats..................**32**

3.4 Order of Format Labels Output **34**

3.5 Example of Using the INVALUE Statement.................................**36**
    3.5.1 JUST and UPCASE Invalue Options.......................................**38**

3.6 Rules for Using VALUE and INVALUE Statements.........................**40**
    3.6.1 Format and Informat Names **41**
    3.6.2 Length of Format and Informat Names **42**
    3.6.3 Format and Informat Name Options **42**
    3.6.4 Additional Label Specifications for Informats.........................**44**
    3.6.5 Specifying Values and Invalues **45**

3.7 Embedded (or Nested) Formats and Informats within Labels **48**

4 PICTURE Statements **51**

4.1 Chapter Overview..**52**

4.2 Digit Selectors in Label Definitions...**52**

4.3 Example: Printing Percentages in PROC TABULATE **53**

4.4 Using the ROUND Option **55**

4.5 PREFIX Option: An Example Using Negative Values **56**

4.6 Specifying Label Widths for **Picture** Formats...............................**56**

4.7 Controlling the Length of the **Picture** Format Label **58**

4.8 Using Internal SAS Formats to Meet Your Needs...............................**59**

4.9 The MULTIPLIER Option **60**

4.10 Additional Options to Use with the PICTURE Statement **63**

5 DATA Step Applications **65**

5.1 Chapter Overview..**66**

5.2 Table Lookup Variable Assignment...**66**

5.3 Two-Dimensional Table Lookup **68**

5.4 Using PUTC and PUTN with Macro Variables.................................**70**

5.5 Using PROC FORMAT to Extract Data **72**

5.6 Using PROC FORMAT for Data Merges: Creating Formats from Data.........**72**

5.7 Applying DATA Step Formats to Outlier Trimming **75**

6 MULTILABEL Option: When One-to-One or Many-to-One Is Not Enough .. **81**

6.1 Chapter Overview **82**

6.2 MULTILABEL Example **83**

7 Managing Format Catalogs **89**

7.1 Chapter Overview **90**

7.2 Storing Formats **90**

7.3 Viewing Stored Formats **92**

7.4 Viewing and Modifying the Format Catalog **94**

7.5 Transporting Stored Formats **96**

Index **97**

Preface

The FORMAT procedure in SAS is an extremely useful procedure that is often included in most of my source code. I first started using PROC FORMAT to create formats to be used as a table lookup for grouping data in reports. I then started to use PROC FORMAT to aid data set creation and also to define new variables. I also learned to apply the procedure for match-merging large data sets that are not sorted by key variables, and finally learned how to define **Picture** formats to format data in reports.

In this book you will learn how to use SAS internal informats and formats. SAS provides a large number of informats and formats that are used for reading data and formatting output.

After we establish how to use informats and formats, we will learn how to use PROC FORMAT for creating user-defined informats and formats. Many beginning programmers do not make much use of the FORMAT procedure. After learning about SAS internal informats and formats, users often skim over the PROC FORMAT chapter in SAS documentation. After reading this book, you will appreciate the value and functionality that PROC FORMAT provides.

Acknowledgments

This book evolved from a combination of factors—from my own enthusiasm with using SAS and from the enthusiasm of fellow SAS users whom I have had the pleasure to meet and work with over the years. Thanks go to the following people for their encouragement, sharing of knowledge, support, and friendship.

To Donna Faircloth, John West, Tate Renner, Shelly Goodin, Monica McClain, Elizabeth Villani, and Patrice Cherry at SAS for handling the editing, production, design, and marketing of this book.

To the series editor Art Carpenter of California Occidental Consultants, for all his input and support.

To the technical reviewers at SAS, Rick Langston, Mandy Chambers, Lynn Mackay, Marty Hultgren, and Morris Vaughn, for providing valuable input on the overall accuracy of the manuscript.

To all the SAS users I have worked with on a professional level over the many years that I have been using SAS. These include Ming Wang, Sonia Sun, Nish Herat, Robert Ladomirak, and Mariusz Kossarski. Each has provided much support in my professional development and to the evolution of this project.

To Ralph W. Leighton for his encouragement and support of my first NESUG paper of the same title.

Thanks to leaders and members of SAS users groups. Without them, I doubt I would be such a SAS geek.

Thanks to my mother, father, grandmother, brother, and sister for all their love and encouragement.

Finally, to my wife Judith for understanding the hours spent at my computer working on this manuscript. To my son Ricky, for understanding that I had less time to play with him while working on what he called "the serious book." I love you both.

Thank you all!

Jonas

x

Using This Book

The book assumes no knowledge of PROC FORMAT for setting up user-defined informats and formats. The book is meant to be read linearly. You should have working knowledge of the SAS DATA step. The book uses the TABULATE, FREQ, MEANS, and GPLOT procedures to illustrate examples, so knowledge of these procedures is helpful but not entirely necessary.

Chapter 1 introduces SAS internal informats and formats. We review how to use internal informats and formats to read and output data.

Chapter 2 discusses why we use PROC FORMAT. If SAS provides many informats and formats why do we need to create new ones? We look at using PROC FORMAT to build table lookup systems and review data sources used in the book.

Chapter 3 details the specifics of VALUE and INVALUE statements. Rules for setting up user informats and formats are detailed using various examples.

Chapter 4 discusses the PICTURE statement for formatting numbers in reports. Details of setting up **Picture** formats along with options are illustrated with examples.

Chapter 5 looks at data applications of PROC FORMAT. Examples include data extracts and matching large data sets that are not sorted by key variables. The chapter details how to generate the user-defined format from Cntlin data sets.

Chapter 6 looks at the MULTILABEL option introduced in SAS 8.

Chapter 7 reviews working with format catalogs. Examples show how to review statistics of generated formats and how to add descriptive labels to formats.

CHAPTER 1

Introduction to SAS Informats and Formats

1.1 Chapter Overview **2**

1.2 Using SAS Informats **2**
    1.2.1 INPUT Statement **3**
    1.2.2 INPUT Function **7**
    1.2.3 INPUTN and INPUTC Functions..**8**
    1.2.4 ATTRIB and INFORMAT Statements **8**

1.3 Using SAS Formats **9**
    1.3.1 FORMAT Statement in Procedures **10**
    1.3.2 PUT Statement **11**
    1.3.3 PUT Function **13**
    1.3.4 PUTN and PUTC Functions...**14**
    1.3.5 BESTw. Format **14**

1.4 Additional Comments **17**

1.1 Chapter Overview

In this chapter we will review how to use SAS informats and formats. We will first review a number of internal informats and formats that SAS provides, and discuss how these are used to read data into SAS and format output. Some of the examples will point out pitfalls to watch for when reading and formatting data.

1.2 Using SAS Informats

Informats are typically used to read or input data from external files called flat files (text files, ASCII files, or sequential files). The informat instructs SAS on how to read data into SAS variables SAS informats are typically grouped into three categories: character, numeric, and date/time. Informats are named according to the following syntax structure:

Character Informats:	**$INFORMAT**w.
Numeric Informats:	**INFORMAT**w.d
Date/Time Informats:	**INFORMAT**w.

The $ indicates a character informat. **INFORMAT** refers to the sometimes optional SAS informat name. The w indicates the width (bytes or number of columns) of the variable. The d is used for numeric data to specify the number of digits to the right of the decimal place. All informats must contain a decimal point (.) so that SAS can differentiate an informat from a SAS variable.

SAS 9 lists other informat categories besides the three mentioned. Some of these are for reading Asian characters and Hebrew characters. The reader is left to explore these other categories.

SAS provides a large number of informats. The complete list is available in SAS Help and Documentation. In this text, we will review some of the more common informats and how to use them. Check SAS documentation for specifics on reading unusual data.

1.2.1 INPUT Statement

One use of SAS informats is in DATA step code in conjunction with the INPUT statement to read data into SAS variables. The first example we will look at will read a hypothetical data file that contains credit card transaction data. Each record lists a separate transaction with three variables: an ID (account identifier), a transaction date, and a transaction amount. The file looks like this:

ID	Transaction Date	Transaction Amount
124325	08/10/2003	1250.03
7	08/11/2003	12500.02
114565	08/11/2003	5.11

The following program is used to read the data into a SAS data set. Since variables are in fixed starting columns, we can use the column-delimited INPUT statement.

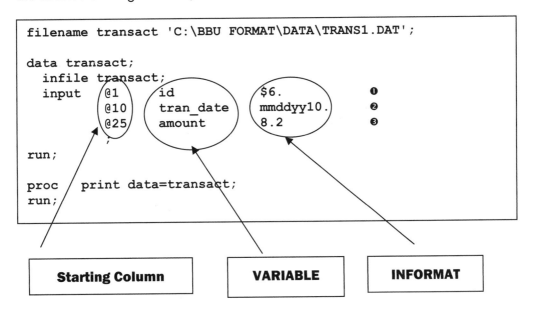

Figure 1.1

The ID variable is read in as a character variable using the **$6.** informat in line ❶. The **$w.** informat tells SAS that the variable is character with a length **w**. The **$w.** informat will also left-justify the variable (leading blanks eliminated). Later in this section we will compare results using the **$CHARw.** informat, which retains leading blanks.

Line ❷ instructs SAS to read in the transaction date (Tran_Date) using the date informat **MMDDYYw.** Since each date field occupies 10 spaces, the w. qualifier is set to 10.

Line ❸ uses the numeric informat **8.2**. The **w.d** informat provides instruction to read the numeric data having a total width of 8 (8 columns) with two digits to the right of the decimal point. SAS will insert a decimal point only if it does not encounter a decimal point in the specified w columns. Therefore, we could have coded the informat as **8.** or **8.2.**

The PROC PRINT output is shown here. Note that the Tran_Date variable is now in terms of SAS date values representing the number of days since the first day of the year specified in the YEARCUTOFF option (for this run, yearcutoff=1920).

```
Obs     id     tran_date     amount

 1     124325     15927      1250.03
 2     7          15928     12500.02
 3     114565     15928         5.11
```

Output 1.1

We can make this example a bit more complicated to illustrate some potential problems that typically arise when reading from flat files. What if the Amount variable contained embedded commas and dollar signs? How would we generate the code to read in these records? Here is the modified data with the code that reads the file using the correct informat instruction:

124325	08/10/2003	$1,250.03
7	08/11/2003	$12,500.02
114565	08/11/2003	5.11

```
filename transact 'C:\BBU FORMAT\DATA\TRANS1.DAT';

data transact;
  infile transact;
  input @1  id         $6.
        @10 tran_date   mmddyy10.
        @25 amount      comma10.2        ❶
        ;
run;

proc print data=transact;
run;
```

Line ❶ uses the numeric informat named **COMMAw.d** to tell SAS to treat the Amount variable as numeric and to strip out leading dollar signs and embedded comma separators. The PROC PRINT output is shown here:

```
Obs     id     tran_date      amount

 1     124325    15927       1250.03
 2     7         15928      12500.02
 3     114565    15928          5.11
```

Output 1.2

Note that the output is identical to the previous run when the data was not embedded with commas and dollar signs. Also note that the width of the informat in the code is now larger (10 as opposed to 8 to account for the extra width taken up by commas and the dollar sign). What seemed like a programming headache was solved simply by using the correct SAS informat. When you come across nonstandard data, always check the documented informats that SAS provides.

Now compare what would happen if we changed the informat for the ID variable from a **$w.** informat to a **$CHARw.** informat. Note that the **$CHARw.** informat will store the variable with leading blanks.

```
filename transact 'C:\BBU FORMAT\DATA\TRANS1.DAT';


data transact;
   infile transact;
   input @1   id          $CHAR6.
         @10 tran_date    mmddyy10.
         @25 amount       comma10.2
         ;
run;

proc print data=transact;
run;
```

Obs	id	tran_date	amount
1	124325	15927	1250.03
2	7	15928	12500.02
3	114565	15928	5.11

Output 1.3

Note that the ID variable now retains leading blanks and is right-justified in the output.

1.2.2 INPUT Function

You can use informats in an INPUT function within a DATA step. As an example, we can convert the ID variable used in the previous example from a character variable to a numeric variable in a subsequent DATA step. The code is shown here:

```
data transact2;
   set transact;
   id_num = input(id,6.);                     ❶

proc print data=transact2;
run;
```

The INPUT function in line ❶ returns the numeric variable Id_Num. The line states that the ID variable is six columns wide and assigns the numeric variable, Id_Num, by using the numeric **w.d** informat. Note that when using the INPUT function, we do not have to specify the *d* component if the character variable contains embedded decimal values. The output of PROC PRINT is shown here. Note that the Id_Num is right-justified as numeric values should be.

Obs	id	tran_date	amount	id_num
1	124325	15927	1250.03	124325
2	7	15928	12500.02	7
3	114565	15928	5.11	114565

Output 1.4

Also note that the resulting informat for the variable assigned using the INPUT function is set to the type of informat used in the argument. In the above example, since **6.** is a numeric informat, the Id_Num variable will be numeric.

1.2.3   INPUTN and INPUTC Functions

The INPUTN and INPUTC functions allow you to specify numeric or character informats at run time. A modified example from SAS 9 Help and Documentation shows how to use the INPUTN function to switch informats that are dependent on values of another variable.

```
options yearcutoff=1920;

data fixdates (drop=start readdate);
   length jobdesc $12 readdate $8;
   input source id lname $ jobdesc $ start $;
   if source=1 then readdate= 'date7.  ';
   else readdate= 'mmddyy8.';
   newdate = inputn(start, readdate);
   datalines;
 1 1604 Ziminski writer 09aug90
 1 2010 Clavell editor 26jan95
 2 1833 Rivera writer 10/25/92
 2 2222 Barnes proofreader 3/26/98
 ;
```

Note that the INPUTC function works like the INPUTN function but uses character informats. Also note that dates are numeric, even though we use special date informats to read the values.

1.2.4   ATTRIB and INFORMAT Statements

The ATTRIB statement can assign the informat in a DATA step. Here is an example of the DATA step in Section 1.2.1 rewritten using the ATTRIB statement:

```
data transact;
   infile transact;
   attrib id        informat=$6.
          tran_date informat=mmddyy10.
          amount    informat=comma10.2
          ;
```

```
input @1  id
      @10 tran_date
      @25 amount
      ;
run;
```

This next example shows how we could also use the INFORMAT statement to read in the data as well. With SAS there is always more than one way to get the job done.

```
data transact;
  infile transact;
  informat id        $6.
           tran_date mmddyy10.
           amount    comma10.2
           ;
  input @1  id
        @10 tran_date
        @25 amount
        ;
run;
```

1.3 Using SAS Formats

If informats are instructions for reading data, then you can view formats as instructions for outputting data. Using the data provided above, we will review how to use some formats that SAS provides.

Since formats are primarily used to format output, we will look at how we can use existing SAS internal formats using the FORMAT statement in PROCs.

1.3.1   FORMAT Statement in Procedures

Return to the first example introduced in Section 1.2.1 and modify PROC PRINT to include a FORMAT statement that would return dates in standard mm/dd/yyyy format and list transaction amounts using dollar signs and commas. Here is the code:

```
options center;
filename transact 'C:\BBU FORMAT\DATA\TRANS1.DAT';

data transact;
  infile transact;
  input @1  id          $6.
        @10 tran_date    mmddyy10.
        @25 amount       8.2
        ;
run;

proc print data=transact;
  format tran_date    mmddyy10.            FORMAT STATEMENT IN PROC
         amount       dollar10.2;
run;
```

Obs	id	tran_date	amount
1	124325	08/10/2003	$1,250.03
2	7	08/11/2003	$12,500.02
3	114565	08/11/2003	$5.11

Output 1.5

Notice that we used a **DOLLARw.d** format to write out the Amount variable with a dollar sign and comma separators. If we used a **COMMAw.d** format, the results would be similar but without the dollar sign. We see that the **COMMAw.d** informat used in Section 1.2.1 has a different function from the **COMMAw.d** format. The informat ignores dollar signs and commas while the **COMMAw.d** format outputs data with embedded commas without the dollar sign. Check SAS Help and Documentation when using informats and formats since the same-named informat may have a different functionality from the same-named format.

1.3.2 PUT Statement

Informats combined with INPUT statements read in data from flat files. Conversely, we can use formats with the PUT statement to write out flat files. Let's see how to take the Transact SAS data set and write out a new flat file using PUT statements. Recall that the Transact data set was created using the following code:

```
options center;
filename transact 'C:\BBU FORMAT\DATA\TRANS1.DAT';

data transact;
   infile transact;
   input @1   id         $6.
         @10  tran_date  mmddyy10.
         @25  amount     8.2
         ;
   run;
```

Run the following code to create a new flat file called transact_out.dat:

```
data _null_;                              ❶
   set transact;                          ❷
   file 'c:\transact_out.dat';            ❸
   put @1   id         $char6.            ❹
       @10  tran_date  mmddyy10.
       @25  amount     8.2
       ;
   run;
```

Some comments about the above code:

❶ The data set name _NULL_ is a special keyword. The _NULL_ data set does not get saved into the workspace. The keyword turns off all the default automatic output that normally occurs at the end of the DATA step. It is used typically for writing output to reports or files.

❷ Use the SET statement to read the transact data into the DATA step.

❸ Specify the output flat file using the FILE statement. Review SAS documentation for FILE statement options for specific considerations (i.e., specifying record lengths for long files, file delimiters, and/or outputting to other platforms such as spreadsheets).

❹ Specify the **$CHARw.** format, but since the ID variable is already left-justified using the **$w.** informat, the output would be the same if a **$w.** format had been used.

The data file created from the above code is shown here:

```
124325    08/10/2003        1250.03
7         08/11/2003       12500.02
114565    08/11/2003           5.11
```

Output 1.6

If the user of the file requires the ID variable to be right-justified, the following changes to the code can accommodate that request. In this code, a new numeric variable called Id_Num was created, which applies the INPUT function to the character ID variable.

```
data _null_;
  set transact;
  file 'c:\transact_out.dat';
  id_num = input(id,6.);
  put @1  id_num    6.
      @10 tran_date mmddyy10.
      @25 amount    8.2
      ;
run;
```

```
124325    08/10/2003        1250.03

     7    08/11/2003       12500.02

114565    08/11/2003           5.11
```

What if the user calls back requesting that the ID variable have leading zeros? This is not a problem because SAS has a special numeric format to include leading zeros called **Zw.d.** Here is the modified code and the output file:

```
data _null_;
  set transact;
  file 'c:\transact_out.dat';
  id_num = input(id,6.);
  put @1  id_num    z6.
      @10 tran_date mmddyy10.
      @25 amount    8.2
      ;
run;
```

124325	08/10/2003	1250.03
000007	08/11/2003	12500.02
114565	08/11/2003	5.11

The above example is handy to have. Especially if you read zip code data as numeric and then want to output results with leading zeros in flat files, reports, or PROCs.

1.3.3 PUT Function

Like the INPUT function, SAS also has the PUT function to use with SAS variables and formats to return character variables. The format applied to the source variable must be the same type as the source variable—numeric or character.

For example, what if we have a data set with a 13-digit numeric variable called Accn_Id and we want to generate a character variable called Char_Accn_Id from the numeric variable with leading zeros? The following PUT function can be applied in a DATA step:

```
char_accn_id = put(accn_id,z13.);
```

Note that the PUT function always returns a character variable while the INPUT function returns a type (numeric or character) dependent on the informat used in the argument.

1.3.4   PUTN and PUTC Functions

These functions work like the INPUTN and INPUTC functions reviewed in Section 1.2.2. The functions allow you to name a format during run time. A detailed example is shown in Chapter 5, Section 5.3.

1.3.5   BESTw. Format

When outputting numeric data without a format specification, SAS uses the default **BESTw.** format. You can increase the width of the numeric display by overriding the default **BESTw.** format by explicitly declaring a **BESTw.** format in a format specification.

To make the concept clear, we'll look at the problem of converting character to numeric data that was introduced in Section 1.2.2. The INPUT function can be used to convert character data to numeric. Here is another example and code:

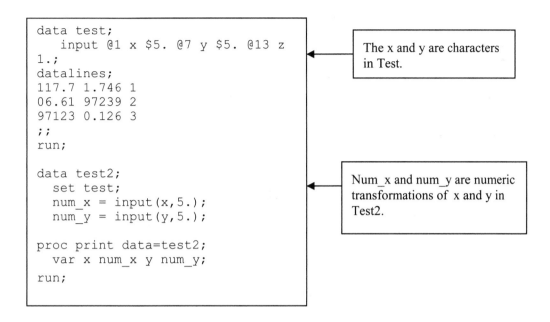

```
data test;
   input @1 x $5. @7 y $5. @13 z
1.;
datalines;
117.7 1.746 1
06.61 97239 2
97123 0.126 3
;;
run;

data test2;
   set test;
   num_x = input(x,5.);
   num_y = input(y,5.);

proc print data=test2;
   var x num_x y num_y;
run;
```

The x and y are characters in Test.

Num_x and num_y are numeric transformations of x and y in Test2.

Figure 1.2

When we look at the output of the run we get the following results, which at first look strange:

Obs	x	num_x	y	num_y
1	117.7	117.70	1.746	1.75
2	06.61	6.61	97239	97239.00
3	97123	97123.00	0.126	0.13

Output 1.7

It looks like the X variable translated correctly, but when we look at the Y variable we notice that digits got rounded off in the Num_y variable. Before blaming the INPUT function in creation of data set Test2, try to increase the width of the numeric display using a **BESTw.** format. Here are the code and output:

```
proc print data=test2;
   var x num_x y num_y;
   format num_y best10.;
run;
```

Obs	x	num_x	y	num_y
1	117.7	117.70	1.746	1.746
2	06.61	6.61	97239	97239
3	97123	97123.00	0.126	0.126

Output 1.8

With the **BESTw.** format applied, we see that the character-to-numeric translation was done correctly.

We can apply the **BESTw.** format to all numeric variables as shown in the following change of PROC PRINT, which formats all numeric data in the data set with the best10. format:

```
proc print data=test2;
   var x num_x y num_y;
   format _numeric_ best10.;
run;
```

Obs	x	num_x	y	num_y
1	117.7	117.7	1.746	1.746
2	06.61	6.61	97239	97239
3	97123	97123	0.126	0.126

Output 1.9

1.4 Additional Comments

There are a large number of informats and formats supplied by SAS. Be clear about your data and the format of your data. Don't assume anything. Always check your SAS logs for warnings and errors. Be on the lookout for incorrect *w* or *d* specifications. If you don't specify large enough widths, character variables will be truncated and numeric data might be reformatted.

As a review of this chapter, the following table shows the function and usage of informats and formats:

CONCEPT	FUNCTION	USAGE IN A DATA STEP	USAGE IN A PROC
INFORMAT	Input data.	Use with the INPUT, ATTRIB, or INFORMAT statement. Use with the INPUT, INPUTN, or INPUTC function.	INFORMAT statements are rarely used in PROCs. Exceptions are PROCs that are used to input data such as PROC FSEDIT.
FORMAT	Output data or format data in reports.	Use with the PUT, ATTRIB, or FORMAT statement. Use with the PUT, PUTC, or PUTN function.	Use the ATTRIB or FORMAT statement.

More Information

More information about SAS informats and formats can be found in SAS Help and Documentation.

CHAPTER 2

Why Use PROC FORMAT?

2.1 Chapter Overview...**20**

2.2 Table Lookups...**20**
    2.2.1 Binary Search Algorithm Used by SAS to Evaluate User-Defined Formats and
    Informats **22**

2.3 Data Sets Used in the Book **22**
    2.3.1 Adult Growth Hormone Deficiency Survey Data.......................................**23**
    2.3.2 Hypothetical Credit Score Data...**25**

2.1 Chapter Overview

Since SAS provides many informats and formats, why would you bother with PROC FORMAT to generate new ones? The primary reason for using PROC FORMAT is to create a table lookup. A common application of a table lookup is to translate codes into everyday terminology. We will introduce the concept of table lookups in this chapter.

In this chapter we will also look at how SAS searches the table lookup built with PROC FORMAT.

We'll finish the chapter by introducing the data we use throughout the book.

2.2 Table Lookups

PROC FORMAT is an excellent tool to build user-defined table lookups. A table lookup is a common programming convention that maps input "values" to output "labels." Values can be either numeric or character. User-defined formats and informats are created using PROC FORMAT and are called later within a DATA step and/or within subsequent PROCs.

In most uses of PROC FORMAT, you will want to utilize either a **one-to-one** or a **many-to-one** mapping. We look at two examples of one-to-one mapping that illustrate the need for mapping coded values into literals. The first example maps values for a one-byte variable named Sex into literals labels that will be used for reporting.

SEX VALUES	MAPPING LABELS
M	MALE
F	FEMALE

The second example comes from a hypothetical credit card application processing reporting system. A one-byte Status variable represents status codes for applicants applying for a credit card. The mapping will be useful for reporting statistics for each status. Here is the conceptual framework for the table:

STATUS VALUES	MAPPING LABELS
A	Approved
D	Declined
P	Pending
C	Canceled by Applicant

The advantage of the table is that we can store the one-byte Status variable in the data set and use the literal mappings in generating reports. This saves space and resources since only the one-byte status field is saved in the SAS data set. Saving the above table takes few resources and the table lookup can apply labels for codes in a subsequent report.

Expanding on the previous example, we might have many codes that map into single labels. The following example illustrates the concept of a many-to-one mapping table lookup.

STATUS VALUES	MAPPING LABELS
A01,A02,A03	Approved
D01,DDF	Declined
P	Pending
C1,C2	Canceled by Applicant

The advantage of table lookup systems is that we don't need to generate new data sets with new variables that describe labels for codes and/or specify regroupings of values into new labels. You can save time and resources with table lookups by avoiding the need to code additional DATA steps. The table lookup system will handle the grouping in the report generation.

By default, PROC FORMAT allows only for a one-to-one or a many-to-one mapping. This is a good feature. If we build a table lookup using IF-THEN/ELSE or IF-THEN statements in a DATA step, there is no guarantee that we will avoid coding-interpretation errors where the same value receives more than one label referenced in the code. For example, we don't get warning messages in the following DATA step, but it is unclear what the mapping should be for a code value of "D01":

```
data app;
   set transact;
   if code in ('A01' 'A02' 'A03' 'D01') then status = 'APPROVE';
   if code in ('D01' 'DDF')            then status = 'DECLINE';
```

The code value of "D01" in the above code gets mapped to the value of "DECLINE." If, however, we started the second IF statement with an ELSE IF, the value "D01" would be mapped to a value of "APPROVE." When we use PROC FORMAT the above error will be flagged in the log.

There is a PROC FORMAT option that would allow many-to-many mappings (MULTILABEL) that will be reviewed in Chapter 6.

2.2.1   *Binary Search Algorithm Used by SAS to Evaluate User-Defined Formats and Informats*

SAS uses a special binary search algorithm when evaluating the format created by PROC FORMAT. When a user generates a user-defined table lookup using PROC FORMAT, the format or informat is stored in memory. A binary search on values is applied when an informat or format is evaluated. The algorithm is more efficient than other table lookup procedures such as IN statements. More information is available in a paper by Perry Watts titled "On the Relationship between Format Structure and Efficiency in SAS."

2.3   Data Sets Used in the Book

Most of the data sources used in the text are simple data sets introduced before each example. There are two additional data sources that are listed here. The first is from an online survey conducted in 2002 of adults diagnosed with adult growth hormone deficiency. The second data set is a hypothetical credit score data set generated with random data. Both of these data sets are reviewed here.

2.3.1 Adult Growth Hormone Deficiency Survey Data

An online survey was conducted in 2002 of adults with diagnosed adult growth hormone deficiency (AGHD). Growth hormone deficiency has many causes, including pituitary tumors, head trauma, congenital defects, pituitary trauma during labor (Sheehan's Syndrome), and no identifiable cause (idiopathic). A subset of the data is used in this book to illustrate PROC FORMAT. Fifty-three subjects participated in the survey.

Here are the data elements for this data:

VARIABLE	DESCRIPTION
dosage	Dosage of growth hormone
age	Age of respondent
agediag	Age diagnosed
agestart	Age start treatment
cause	Cause of AGHD
diag_as_child	Diagnosis made as a child (Y=YES, N=NO)?
happy_endo	Is respondent happy with his/her doctor (Y=YES, N=NO)?
mstat	Marital status
number_of_surgeries	number of brain tumor (pituitary or other) surgeries
rad	Received radiation treatment (Y=YES, N=NO)?
sat	How satisfied respondent is with treatment
sex	M=Male, F=Female
state	State of residence

The code used to generate the data is provided here:

```
libname bbu "C:\SAS BBU Format\DATA";

data bbu.aghd;
input @ 1 dosage
      @10 age
      @15 agediag
      @20 agestart
      @25 cause $12.
      @40 diag_as_child  $1.
      @45 happy_endo  $1.
      @50 mstat  $1.
      @55 number_surgeries
      @60 rad   $1.
      @65 sat   $1.
      @70 sex   $1.
      @75 state $2.
      ;

datalines;
0.7143   46    7   41   1        Y   Y   M   2   Y   5   M   CT
0.8      51   49   50   2        N   Y   M       .   5   M   NY
0.3       .   13   30   3        Y   Y   S       .   5   F   IN
0.6      51   12   51   2        Y   Y   M       .   5   M   CA
0.4      29   27   27   1        N   Y   S   1   Y   5   F   FL
0.7      35   11   32   3        Y   Y   M       .   5   F   CA
.        53   49   50   4        N   Y   S       .   5   F   OR
0.4      54   48   51   5        N   Y   M       .   5   F   OR
0.4      38   38   38   3        N   N   M       .   5   F   TX
0.6      46   46   46   4        N   Y   M       .   5   F   KY
0.3      31   23   29   1        N   N   S   1   Y   4   M   XX
0.6      41   40   40   1        N   Y   M   1   N   5   F   WI
.        17   14    .   2        Y   Y   S       .   5   F   OH
.        18   11   11   1        Y   N   S       .   Y   5   F   GA
.        39    8    .   2        Y   N   D       .   5   F   MI
.         .    .    .            Y   Y   S       .   5   F   XX
0.8      65   19   60   4        N   Y   M       .   5   F   TX
0.6      49   48   48   1        N   Y   M   2   N   5   F   AR
0.02     19   18   18   3        N   Y   S       .   3   M   PA
0.5      37   37   37   1        N   Y   M   2   N   4   F   IN
0.28     28    7    5   1        Y   Y   S   1   N   4   M   MO
.        44   40   41   4        N   N   M       .   4   F   NY
.        61    5   61   2        Y   Y   W       .   3   M   HI
0.5      28   26   26   4        N   Y   M       .   5   F   TX
0.8      52   50   50   3        N   Y   S       .   5   F   MO
0.06     30   29   29   6        N   Y   M       .   4   F   CA
0.4      40   29   38   4        N   Y   M       .   4   F   MN
0.6      46   45   45   4        N   Y   M   0       5   F   SC
0.8      49   45   48   1        N   Y   M   1   Y   5   F   FL
0.4      37   37   37   6        N   N   S       .   4   F   CA
```

```
.        45   45   45   4        N    Y    M    .         3    F    IL
.        61   56   56   4        N    Y    M    .         5    F    TX
0.54     20    8   18   1        Y    Y    S    1    N    4    F    WI
0.08     22    3   19   3        Y    Y    S    .         4    M    GA
0.0002   50   50   50   1        N    Y    S    1    N    5    M    IN
0.3      23   15   16   1        Y    Y    S    1    N    5    M    NJ
0.6      40   35   39   1        N    Y    M    1    Y    3    F    RI
0.8      52   52   52   1        N    Y    M    1    N    2    F    ID
.        32   30    .   1        N    N    S    1    N    5    M    NY
0.4      46   44   45   1        N    Y    D    1    N    5    M    VA
.        53    .    .   1        N    N    M    0    N    1    F    MD
0.7      35   16   18   1        Y    Y    M    1    N    5    F    XX
.        24    .    .   1        Y    N    S    1    N    1    F    WI
0.6      40   38   38   1        N    Y    D    0    N    5    M    MI
0.8      42   40   41   1        N    Y    D    2    Y    4    M    MN
1        32   31   31   1        N    Y    M    1    N    5    F    KY
.        32   16   27   1        Y    N    S    1    N    1    F    CA
0.4      27   26   26   1        N    Y    S    1    N    4    M    XX
0.6      23    1    1   2        Y    Y    M    .         5    F    NH
0.6      70   68   68   3        N    Y    S    .         4    M    MO
.        30   23   23   1        N    Y    M    1    N    4    F    FL
.        39   38   38   2        N    Y    S    .         5    F    NY
0.4      35   16   34   1        Y    Y    S    1    N    5    F    WA
;;;
run;
```

Note that values of "XX" for the state variable represent missing states or international addresses.

2.3.2 Hypothetical Credit Score Data

Using SAS random functions, simulated data were generated to mimic consumer credit score data. The data include prediction scores for risk (Score) and income (Income_Est). The data set also contains a bad risk indicator variable (Bad) that indicates if an account went severely delinquent within a 12-month period after being scored. A total of 10,000 observations were generated using random functions and functional equations. Here are the data elements:

VARIABLE	DESCRIPTION
ID	Unique identifier key.
score	Integer score predictive of risk. The higher the score, the less likely the account will default.
income_est	Income prediction.
bad	(0,1) If 1, account is tagged as bad (delinquent).

The source code used to generate the data is provided here:

```
data bbu.scores;
  do id = 1 to 10000;
    x = rannor(98);
    score = INT(196 +16*x);
    lnest = -5.322033893 + 0.034657359*score;
    pbad = exp(lnest)/(exp(lnest)+1);
    a = ranuni(56);
    bad = (a>pbad);
    income_est = INT(15000 <> (-130948.5714 + 905.1428571*score +
                  rannor(4)*5500));
    drop x a pbad lnest;
    output;
  end;
run;
```

More Information
Watts, P. 2001. "On the Relationship between Format Structure and Efficiency in SAS." *Proceedings of the Fourteenth Annual NorthEast SAS Users Group Conference*, Baltimore, MD, 697-705.   More information about growth hormone deficiency in adults and children can be obtained from the MAGIC Foundation (www.magicfoundation.org, 1-800-3-MAGIC-3).

CHAPTER 3

VALUE and INVALUE Statements: Syntax and Examples

3.1 Chapter Overview **28**

3.2 Introductory Example **28**
    3.2.1 Using the IF-THEN/ELSE Statement **29**
    3.2.2 Using the VALUE Statement... **30**

3.3 Internal SAS Character Informats and Impact on User-Defined Formats **32**

3.4 Order of Format Labels Output **34**

3.5 Example of Using the INVALUE Statement **36**
    3.5.1 JUST and UPCASE Invalue Options...................................... **38**

3.6 Rules for Using VALUE and INVALUE Statements.................................. **40**
    3.6.1 Format and Informat Names **41**
    3.6.2 Length of Format and Informat Names **42**
    3.6.3 Format and Informat Name Options **42**
    3.6.4 Additional Label Specifications for Informats......................... **44**
    3.6.5 Specifying Values and Invalues **45**

3.7 Embedded (or Nested) Formats and Informats within Labels **48**

3.1 Chapter Overview

PROC FORMAT has three primary statements—VALUE, INVALUE, and PICTURE. The VALUE and PICTURE statements are used to generate user-defined formats while the INVALUE statement is used to generate informats. This chapter will detail the syntax of the VALUE and INVALUE statements with illustrative examples. Chapter 4 will focus on the use of the PICTURE statement.

We begin the chapter by reviewing how to set up descriptive labels for variable values. The first example uses a DATA step to define a new variable as a function of an existing variable we want to report on. The second example shows how the process would be handled by setting up a table lookup using the PROC FORMAT VALUE statement.

We then review the lengths of values and how variables are stored in SAS. Specific discussion looks at internal formats **$w.** and **$CHARw.**

The order of output with PROC FORMAT is reviewed next. We show how to change the order of labels in report output.

An example of using the INVALUE statement is reviewed next. We then list and detail rules for using the INVALUE and VALUE statements. We finish the chapter by showing you how to embed formats and informats within labels.

3.2 Introductory Example

The data used in this chapter come from an online survey of adult patients diagnosed with growth hormone deficiency. The examples look at descriptive sample characteristics of responders (sex, age, age diagnosed, dosage of growth hormone). The first example generates a frequency report of the number of male and female responders. The first attempt is made using IF-THEN/ELSE logic in a DATA step.

3.2.1 Using the IF-THEN/ELSE Statement

The following code assigns labels for the Sex variable using a DATA step:

```
options nocenter errors=2;
libname bbu "C:\SAS BBU Format\DATA";

data example1;
  set bbu.Aghd;
  if sex='M' then sexg='Male';
  else sexg='Female';

proc freq data=example1;
  tables sexg;
run;
```

sexg	Frequency	Percent	Cumulative Frequency	Cumulative Percent
Fema	37	69.81	37	69.81
Male	16	30.19	53	100.00

Output 3.1

Notice that records with a sex value of "F" ended up with a label "Fema" in the report as opposed to "Female." Since the length of the Sexg variable was not specified, it gets set at the first execution of the assignment. Since the first record in the data set was a male, the length of the Sexg variable was set to 4 bytes. Subsequent "F" records were truncated to "Fema." Of course there are a number of DATA step solutions to this problem, but we'll investigate how a simple user-defined format can generate the frequency report.

3.2.2 Using the VALUE Statement

Let's see how PROC FORMAT can be used to set up a table lookup to provide a label for the **sex** values. PROC FORMAT uses the keyword VALUE to set up user-defined formats mapping values to labels. The syntax structure of PROC FORMAT for user-defined formats is as follows:

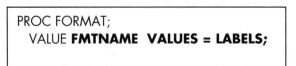

```
PROC FORMAT;
   VALUE FMTNAME  VALUES = LABELS;
```

Figure 3.1

Rules for defining format names **(FMTNAME)** are outlined in Section 3.6. For this introductory example, note that format names for character variables must begin with a **$** since we want to assign a format to the character variable, Sex. The code that will set up the user-defined format is shown here:

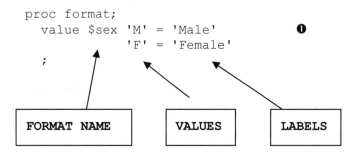

```
proc format;
   value $sex 'M' = 'Male'              ❶
              'F' = 'Female'
   ;
```

| FORMAT NAME | VALUES | LABELS |

Figure 3.2

We then apply the user-defined format in a PROC FREQ. In this example, we avoid the need to generate a new data set to assign the label as was done in Section 3.2.1. This saves resources for both data storage and CPU time. The code is shown here:

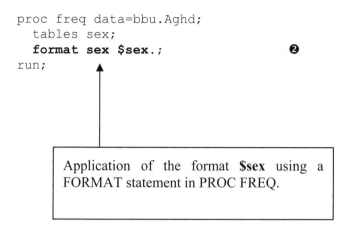

```
proc freq data=bbu.Aghd;
   tables sex;
   format sex $sex.;                        ❷
run;
```

Application of the format **$sex** using a
FORMAT statement in PROC FREQ.

```
The FREQ Procedure

                                 Cumulative    Cumulative
sex        Frequency    Percent   Frequency     Percent

Female          37      69.81         37         69.81     ❸
Male            16      30.19         53        100.00
```

Output 3.2

❶ The user-defined format is named **$sex.** The name of the format is up to the user and
does not have to be the same as the variable that it will be assigned to. Format names
and variables are independent of each other and a format must be explicitly assigned to a
variable in subsequent PROC or DATA steps. Also note that since Sex is a character
variable, the user format starts with a "$" to designate that the format is a character
format. In this example, "M" maps to "Male" and "F" maps to "Female."

❷ An additional DATA step was not required to assign labels. The application of the
user-defined format must be explicitly assigned in the PROC with a FORMAT statement.
Here Sex is output using the user-defined format **$sex**. The format assignment ends with a
period. This is identical to using internal SAS formats.

❸ Looking at the output, note that now the "Female" label is correctly outputted in the frequency report. This was not the case with the IF-THEN/ELSE solution to the problem.

3.3 Internal SAS Character Informats and Impact on User-Defined Formats

How data are stored in your SAS data set will affect how user-defined formats are evaluated. Let's take a look at another example where the Sex variable is stored as a two-byte character variable. Female responders are coded as "Fe" while male responders are coded as "M." We want to test the format **$sx.**, which is defined as shown:

```
proc format;
   value $sx   'Fe' = 'Female'
               'M'  = 'Male'
   ;
```

When we read the Sex variable, we can specify one of many character informats. In this example, we will look at reading Sex using the **$w.** and the **$CHARw.** informats. Recall from Section 1.2.1 that the **$w.** informat will left-justify values while the **$CHARw.** informat will retain leading spaces. Let's look at an example using the **$w.** informat to store the variable.

```
data test;
   input sex $2.;
   datalines;
Fe
 M
Fe
Fe
 M
 M
;


proc freq data=test;
   table sex;
   format sex $sx.;
run;
```

sex	Frequency	Percent	Cumulative Frequency	Cumulative Percent
Female	3	50.00	3	50.00
Male	3	50.00	6	100.00

Output 3.3

Notice that even though the Sex variable is a two-byte character field, we specified only a single byte for the "M" value in the PROC FORMAT value definition. Since the variable is read in using the **$w.** informat, the value gets left-justified.

Look at how the format will work if we read the Sex variable using a **$CHARw.** informat.

```
data test2;
   input sex $char2.;
   datalines;
Fe
 M
Fe
Fe
 M
 M
;
proc freq data=test2;
   table sex;
   format sex $sx.; run;
```

The FREQ Procedure				
sex	Frequency	Percent	Cumulative Frequency	Cumulative Percent
M	3	50.00	3	50.00
Female	3	50.00	6	100.00

Output 3.4

The **$CHARw.** informat does not left-justify fields the way the **$w.** informat does. As a result, the Sex value for males is stored as " M" in data set Test2. Since that value was not specified in the format, the value does not get formatted in the application of the user-defined **$sx.** format.

To solve this problem, modify the user-defined value format to include leading spaces in the value for males:

```
proc format;
   value $sx   'Fe'       = 'Female'
               'M',' M'   = 'Male'
   ;

proc freq data=test;   /* DATA using $2. */      ❶
   table sex;
   format sex $sx.;
run;
proc freq data=test2; /* DATA using $CHAR2. */ ❷
   table sex;
   format sex $sx.;
run;
```

```
The FREQ Procedure

                                  Cumulative    Cumulative
sex          Frequency    Percent   Frequency      Percent

Female            3        50.00           3        50.00      ❶
Male              3        50.00           6       100.00

The FREQ Procedure

                                  Cumulative    Cumulative
sex          Frequency    Percent   Frequency      Percent

Male              3        50.00           3        50.00      ❷
Female            3        50.00           6       100.00
```

Output 3.5

Note that the data set Test (❶) was generated using the SAS❷ informat **$w.** while Test2 (❷) was generated with the application of the **$CHARw.** informat. Also note that the two runs of PROC FREQ generated two different orderings of the Sex variable in the output. The next section will review how to specify a specific ordering of labels in your reports.

3.4 Order of Format Labels Output

By default, certain procedures such as FREQ and TABULATE output data sorted by the internal values of the variable. In the first data set, "Fe" comes before "M" since the **$w.** informat left-justifies the field. The second data set has the male indicator of " M" sorted first since the field contains a blank in the first position retained by the **$CHARw.** informat. The " M" value comes before the "Fe" value, resulting in the "Male" label being listed first in the output.

To have the output sorted by the user-defined format, use the ORDER=FORMATTED option. Application and output are shown here.

```
proc freq data=test2 ORDER=FORMATTED;
   table sex;
   format sex $sx.;
```

```
The FREQ Procedure

                                    Cumulative   Cumulative
sex           Frequency    Percent   Frequency     Percent

Female            3         50.00        3          50.00
Male              3         50.00        6         100.00
```

Output 3.6

To force a specific order of output, modify labels, and then run the report using ORDER=FORMATTED. Here are two examples using the data above, forcing the "Male" label to appear first. Note that here we define two formats.

```
proc format;
   value $srta 'Fe'      = 'Female'
               'M',' M'  = ' Male'
   ;
   value $srtb 'Fe'      = '2: Female'
               'M',' M'  = '1: Male'
   ;

proc freq data=test ORDER=FORMATTED;
   tables sex;
   format sex $srta.;

proc freq data=test ORDER=FORMATTED;
   tables sex;
   format sex $srtb.;
run;
```

```
The FREQ Procedure

                                  Cumulative    Cumulative
sex          Frequency    Percent  Frequency     Percent

Male              3        50.00        3         50.00
Female            3        50.00        6        100.00

The FREQ Procedure

                                  Cumulative    Cumulative
sex          Frequency    Percent  Frequency     Percent

1: Male           3        50.00        3         50.00
2: Female         3        50.00        6        100.00
```

Output 3.7

An alternative method for ordering output format labels is shown in Section 6.2.

3.5 Example of Using the INVALUE Statement

The INVALUE statement is similar to the VALUE statement. The difference is that the VALUE statement is used for creating SAS formats while the INVALUE statement is used for setting up SAS informats. Recall that informats are instructions to read data while formats are instructions on how to write out the data. Here is the syntax structure of PROC FORMAT for user-defined informats:

```
PROC FORMAT;
    INVALUE INFMTNAME  INVALUES = LABELS;
```

Figure 3.3

One example of using the INVALUE statement is to read in data using a user-specified informat. We will use the DATA step from the example in Section 3.3. This time we use a user-defined informat as opposed to the SAS internal **$w.** or **$CHARw.** informat to read the data. Examples of code and output follow:

```
proc format;
   invalue $sx  'Fe' = 'Female'
                ' M' = 'Male'
   ;


data informat_test;
   input sex $sx.;    ◄────────────────────
   datalines;
Fe
 M
Fe
Fe
 M
 M
;

proc print data=informat_test;
run;
```

> We use the user-defined informat **$sx** to read the Sex variable instead of **$w.** or **$CHARw.**

Obs	sex
1	Female
2	Male
3	Female
4	Female
5	Male
6	Male

Output 3.8

The default length of the variable is determined by the specification of the informat. The default length of the informat (or format) is determined by the longest label if the label is character. If the value or invalue is numeric (unquoted), the length is set to 12. You can override the default length by using the DEFAULT=*length* option applied to the informat or format name. The next section shows you how to use a few other options with the specification of informats.

3.5.1   JUST and UPCASE Invalue Options

The INVALUE statement has some additional options that can operate on the variable invalues before applying the informat. The JUST option will left-justify invalues before applying the informat. The UPCASE option will convert invalues of the variable to uppercase before applying the informat.

A new example using the JUST option with the example from Section 3.5 is shown here. The output from the DATA step and PROC PRINT is identical. Note that the invalue definition for "M" is now left-justified since the JUST option forces a left-justification of the values before applying the informat. This is a helpful option.

```
proc format;
   invalue $sx (just) 'Fe' = 'Female'
                      'M'  = 'Male'
   ;
```

Let's see how the UPCASE option will work. Remember that the option applies to the values and not the labels. For the example, we will apply both options, JUST and UPCASE. I changed the data a bit by making one of the "M" invalues for Sex lowercase. Code and output are shown here:

```
proc format;
   invalue $sx (just upcase)
               'FE' = 'Female'
               'M'  = 'Male'
   ;

data informat_test;
   input sex $sx.;
   datalines;
Fe
 M
Fe
Fe
 m
 M
;

proc print data=informat_test;
run;
```

The example in Section 3.5 listed the invalue as "Fe."

The example in Section 3.5 listed the invalue as " M."

I changed one of the "M" data invalues to an "m."

```
                    Obs     sex

                     1      Female
                     2      Male
                     3      Female
                     4      Female
                     5      Male
                     6      Male
```

Output 3.9

What would happen if we accidentally coded the last invalue example without listing all the invalues in capital letters? Here is an example:

```
proc format;
   invalue $sx (just upcase)
               'Fe' = 'Female'
               'M'  = 'Male'
   ;
```

The output from PROC PRINT generates these results:

```
                        Obs    sex

                         1     Fe
                         2     Male
                         3     Fe
                         4     Fe
                         5     Male
                         6     Male
```

Output 3.10

Why did the value of "Fe" output as "Fe"? With the UPCASE option, all variable invalues are converted to uppercase before applying the informat. Therefore, the invalue "Fe" is converted to "FE" before mapping to a label. However, our informat specification did not include a mapping for the invalue "FE." As a result, the invalue "FE" does not map to any labels and the original invalue is returned.

This feature is also true for user-defined formats. Any variable value not listed in the values specification will not format, and the original variable value is returned.

3.6 Rules for Using VALUE and INVALUE Statements

We have seen from the previous examples that when using PROC FORMAT to specify user formats or informats, the VALUE or INVALUE statement has three components. These components are the format or informat name **(FMTNAME** or **INFMTNAME)**, the specification of the values or invalues, and a resulting mapping to labels. In this section we will detail some of the rules for creating user-defined informats and formats.

```
PROC FORMAT;
    VALUE      FMTNAME      VALUES = LABELS;
    INVALUE INFMTNAME INVALUES = LABELS;
```

Figure 3.4

3.6.1 Format and Informat Names

Every character **FMTNAME** and **INFMTNAME** must begin with a "$." The choice for determining whether a character or numeric format is required depends on the actual variable that the format or informat is being applied to. If a **FMTNAME** begins with a "$," it indicates a character designation, otherwise the numeric format or informat is assumed.

The name of the format or informat cannot begin or end with numbers. If you try to set up a format or informat with starting or ending numbers, SAS will return an error message. In Section 5.6 we set up formats directly from special data sets. We have to make sure the variables from the data set do not start or end with numbers. The example in Section 5.7 will show how to pad special characters to the beginning and end of each variable name to avoid the potential error.

You cannot use names that are used by SAS internal formats or informats. The **FMTNAME** and **INFMTNAME** do not have to match the name of an existing variable. User-defined formats and informats are independent of the data variable names. User-defined formats and informats are defined first and then applied to variables in subsequent PROC or DATA steps.

You can include many VALUE and INVALUE statements as required with just one invocation of the PROC FORMAT statement. You can mix VALUE and INVALUE statements as well in one PROC FORMAT.

3.6.2 *Length of Format and Informat Names*

For SAS 9, the maximum length of the format **FMTNAME** is 32 bytes, which includes the "$" if required for character formats. The maximum length of the informat **INFMTNAME** is 31 bytes. If you define a character informat, the "$" is included in the determination of the maximum length. SAS releases prior to SAS 9 have a maximum **FMTNAME** length of 8 and a maximum **INFMTNAME** length of 7.

3.6.3 *Format and Informat Name Options*

There are a number of options available when defining formats and informats. To view all options, refer to SAS Help and Documentation. We used the JUST and UPCASE options in Section 3.5.1. Here are some other options that can be helpful when defining your formats or informats. These options appear in parentheses after the name of the format or informat.

NOTSORTED. By default SAS stores format values or ranges in order and uses a binary search algorithm to locate the range a value falls in. When you specify the NOTSORTED option, SAS searches each range in the order specified. This option can save CPU time if you know that a particular range is more frequent than others and that frequent ranges are specified at the top of the list. For more information about efficiency issues when using PROC FORMAT, see the paper by Perry Watts titled "On the Relationship between Format Structure and Efficiency in SAS."

FUZZ. This option is used to specify a fuzz factor when matching values to ranges. If a value is not in the range but within the fuzz factor, the range is considered a match. Here is an example where we did not use the FUZZ option at first but applied it on the second attempt:

```
data test;
  do test_values = 1/3, 2/3;
    output;
  end;
run;

proc format;
  value testa .3333 = '1/3'
              .6667 = '2/3'
  ;
```

```
   value testb (fuzz=.001) .3333 = '1/3'
                           .6667 = '2/3'
 ;
run;


proc freq data=test;                    ❶
   tables test_values;
   format test_values testa.;
run;

proc freq data=test;                    ❷
   tables test_values;
   format test_values testb.;
run;
```

The FREQ Procedure				❶
test_ values	Frequency	Percent	Cumulative Frequency	Cumulative Percent
.33	1	50.00	1	50.00
.67	1	50.00	2	100.00
The FREQ Procedure				❷
test_ values	Frequency	Percent	Cumulative Frequency	Cumulative Percent
1/3	1	50.00	1	50.00
2/3	1	50.00	2	100.00

Output 3.11

Example ❶ ran without the FUZZ option. Example ❷ applied the FUZZ option to the format and the values printed out as expected in PROC FREQ. This example also shows a useful way to test user formats and informats with a DO step within the DATA step. We will use this technique in Section 4.6 on **Picture** formats to test user-defined **Picture** formats.

Note that a FUZZ option of 0 should be used whenever possible to avoid conflicts of label assignment. Also note that the FUZZ option works only with numeric format **(VALUE** and **PICTURE)** creation.

DEFAULT. The default option is used to specify the default length of the informat or format label. We can also specify the maximum length and minimum length using the MAX and MIN options. Here is an example using the default option to increase the length of nonformatted values in a PROC FREQ output:

```
data test;
  do test_values = 1/3, 2/3, 1/6;
    output;
  end;
run;

proc format;
  value testd (default=6 FUZZ=.001)  .3333 = '1/3'
                                     .6667 = '2/3'
  ;
run;

proc freq data=test;
  tables test_values;
  format test_values testd.;
run;
```

```
The FREQ Procedure

 test_                            Cumulative   Cumulative
 values    Frequency    Percent   Frequency     Percent
 ─────────────────────────────────────────────────────────
 0.1667        1         33.33        1          33.33
 1/3           1         33.33        2          66.67
 2/3           1         33.33        3         100.00
```

Output 3.12

3.6.4 Additional Label Specifications for Informats

For INVALUE statements, there is the informat **LABEL _SAME_** that is used to assign the same values to the data range. There is an additional informat label of **_ERROR_** that is used to flag the value as an error, assign a missing value, and print the data line and warning in the log.

3.6.5 Specifying Values and Invalues

If there is only one value or invalue to be mapped, we list it followed by the mapping label. If there is a range of values or invalues, we can separate them by commas or use specific range specifications that we will review here.

This example generates a frequency distribution of age groupings of responders in the AGHD survey data.

```
proc format;
   value age low - 20   = 'LE 20'     ❶
               21-30     = '21-30'     ❷
               31-40     = '31-40'
               41-50     = '41-50'
               51-60     = '51-60'
               61 - high = 'GT 60'     ❸
                  .      = 'MISSING'   ❹
   ;

proc freq data=bbu.Aghd;
   tables age/missing;                 ❺
   format age age.;
```

Special Values or Invalues

- **Low:**
    - For numeric data, **Low** captures the smallest nonmissing value for numeric formats.
    - For character data, **Low** includes missing values.
    - See observation notes in Section 3.5 for details when using missing values.
- **High:** Highest value.
- **Other:** Other values are not specified. This includes missing values if the values are not already defined in the values or invalues.

Figure 3.5

```
The FREQ Procedure

                                      Cumulative    Cumulative
age         Frequency      Percent    Frequency      Percent
_____
MISSING          2          3.77           2          3.77
LE 20            4          7.55           6         11.32
21-30           10         18.87          16         30.19
31-40           15         28.30          31         58.49
41-50           11         20.75          42         79.25
51-60            7         13.21          49         92.45
GT 60            4          7.55          53        100.00
```

Output 3.13

This format name does not start with a "$" since we want to apply the age format to the numeric Age variable. Again, the name of the format does not have to match the variable that will be formatted, but it often makes for easier association to name the format for the variable we will apply the **VALUE** format to.

Ranges are specified with a "-" separated by endpoint values that are included in the label designation. For line ❷, values from 21 through 30 are formatted as "21-30." The values 21 and 30 are included in the range to be formatted to the label.

Special endpoints are "LOW" and "HIGH." LOW (❶) includes the lowest nonmissing numeric value. HIGH (❺) includes the largest value in the range. For character formats, the LOW designation includes missing values. This is important to remember since, by default, you cannot overlap values into multiple labels. Here is code that shows the incorrect and correct ways to set up a missing character in range specification:

```
21    proc format;
22       value $stuffa ' '        = 'Missing'   /* error set up */
23                  LOW -'C'  = 'Low Values'
24                  'D'-high  = 'High Values'
25       ;
ERROR: These two ranges overlap: LOW-C and - (fuzz=0).
NOTE: The previous statement has been deleted.
26       value $stuffb ' '        = 'Missing'   /* correct set up */
27                  ' ' <-'C' = 'Low Values'
28                  'D'-high  = 'High Values'
29
30       ;
NOTE: Format $STUFFB has been output.
```

Missing values can receive format labels. Missing values for numeric data are represented by default as a period (.), and character missing values are represented with a blank. For this example, missing data receive a label of "MISSING" (❹). If we wanted to include a "MISSING" label in one of our **sex** formats, we would add a missing range to the VALUE statement. This is illustrated here. By using the practice of placing the semicolon (;) on a separate line, we add a new line to the last row of the format definition and add the missing specification.

```
proc format;
   value $sx    'Fe'      = 'Female'
                'M',' M'  = ' Male'
                ' '       = 'MISSING'
   ;
```

To include the missing values and the "MISSING" labels in the frequency report, the MISSING option is added to the TABLES statement (❺). Without this option, SAS would report two missing values after the FREQ report and not include the missing in percent, cumulative frequency, and cumulative percent statistics.

The Age variable is an integer variable. Sometimes we want to generate a format for a variable that is continuous. A second example with ranges is for a dosage of growth hormone:

```
proc format;
   value dosage 0                = '0mg'
                0    < - 0.25 = 'GT 0mg - 0.25mg'       ❶
                0.25 < - 0.50 = 'GT 0.25mg - 0.50mg'
                0.50 < - 0.75 = 'GT 0.50mg - 0.75mg'
                0.75 < - 1    = 'GT 0.75mg - 1.00mg'
                1.00 < - high = 'GT 1.00mg'
                .             = 'MISSING'
                other         = 'Strange Entry'        ❷
   ;
proc freq data=bbu.Aghd;
   tables dosage/missing;
   format dosage dosage.;
run;
```

```
The FREQ Procedure

                                          Cumulative    Cumulative
Dosage                Frequency   Percent  Frequency      Percent

MISSING                      15     28.30         15        28.30
GT  0mg  -  0.25mg            4      7.55         19        35.85
GT  0.25mg - 0.50mg         14     26.42         33        62.26
GT  0.50mg - 0.75mg         13     24.53         46        86.79
GT  0.75mg - 1.00mg          7     13.21         53       100.00
```

Output 3.14

Line ❶ formats ranges from values larger than 0 through 0.25, including 0.25. The < means that the value is not included in the range. Usage rules are as follows:

A < - B :	values larger than A through B, including B
A – B:	values from A through B, including A and B
A - < B:	values from A, including A to all values less than B
A < - < B:	values from A to B, excluding A and B

Values for A and B can be either numeric or character ranges.

You cannot use > in the range specification.

Line ❷ contains the special keyword OTHER. Any range not specified gets labeled with the mapping of the value to "Strange Entry." Note that for the FREQ output, no entries are tagged as "Strange Entry." If missing is not included in the value specification, missing is included in the OTHER range.

3.7 Embedded (or Nested) Formats and Informats within Labels

You can include existing formats or informats within the label. They must be enclosed in brackets or vertical lines enclosed within ()s. Do not enclose the embedded format or informat in quotation marks. The following example counts the number of players winning $1, $5, or $10 in a game of chance. If no money is won, we want to see the output label of "Loser."

```
proc format;
  value win      0 = 'Loser'
             other = [dollar5.]
  ;
proc freq data=win;
  tables win;
  format win win.;
run;
```

```
The FREQ Procedure

                                  Cumulative    Cumulative
   win     Frequency    Percent    Frequency      Percent

Loser          609      60.90          609        60.90
  $1           209      20.90          818        81.80
  $5           138      13.80          956        95.60
 $10            44       4.40         1000       100.00
```

Output 3.15

The dollar format can also be coded as (|dollar5.|) for the above example. Note that you can also include user-defined informats or formats within the embedded label as well.

More Information

More information about PROC FORMAT can be found in SAS Help and Documentation.

Watts, P. 2001. "On the Relationship between Format Structure and Efficiency in SAS." *Proceedings of the Fourteenth Annual NorthEast SAS Users Group Conference*, Baltimore, MD, 697-705.

CHAPTER 4

PICTURE Statements

4.1 Chapter Overview **52**

4.2 Digit Selectors in Label Definitions **52**

4.3 Example: Printing Percentages in PROC TABULATE **53**

4.4 Using the ROUND Option **55**

4.5 PREFIX Option: An Example Using Negative Values **56**

4.6 Specifying Label Widths for **Picture** Formats **56**

4.7 Controlling the Length of the **Picture** Format Label **58**

4.8 Using Internal SAS Formats to Meet Your Needs **59**

4.9 The MULTIPLIER Option **60**

4.10 Additional Options to Use with the PICTURE Statement **63**

4.1 Chapter Overview

Picture formats are templates for printing numbers. They allow you to embed special characters within a number, multiply the number before printing, and control the printing of leading zeros. The syntax structure for a **Picture** format is defined this way:

```
PROC FORMAT;
  PICTURE FMTNAME VALUES = LABELS;
```

Figure 4.1

The structure is similar to the definition of user-defined formats using the VALUE statement in Section 3.2.2. The difference lies in the definition of the labels. The label definition uses digit selectors that indicate how values are formatted when outputted using a PUT or FORMAT statement.

This chapter will define the concept of digit selectors and will show a number of examples of how to use **Picture** formats. We then turn to some of the options for **FMTNAME** for **Picture** formats.

Next we look at the options used with labels. We then finish with a look at how to control the length of **Picture** format output.

4.2 Digit Selectors in Label Definitions

The label template in a **Picture** format contains digit selectors that determine how numbers are displayed. There are two types of digit selectors:

- 0: Placeholders for digits. If a digit exists, a number gets printed. If not, then nothing gets printed.

- 9 (or any digit other than 0): an absolute placeholder that forces a number to print even if it is 0.

For example, if we want to print the number 86, here is how the 86 will appear with different labels:

LABEL	OUTPUT
'0000'	86
'9999'	0086

Figure 4.2

Picture formats can include the thousands separator, a decimal separator, and text or special characters.

4.3 Example: Printing Percentages in PROC TABULATE

The TABULATE procedure has many ways of reporting percentage statistics. The drawback is that the output does not include a percent sign. We will solve that problem by adding the following PICTURE statement to the PROC FORMAT step:

```
picture pct low-high = '009.9%'
;
```

In the example code, note that we include a PICTURE statement and a VALUE statement in one PROC FORMAT. You can add as many VALUE, INVALUE, and PICTURE statements in one PROC FORMAT as you want. The example uses the data generated in Section 2.3.2.

```
proc format;
   value score low-<200 = 'LT 200'
               200-high = 'GT 200'
   ;




   picture pct low-high = '009.9%'
   ;
```

The format **score** defines score groups.

Picture Format pct:

- Includes a forced leading zero to the left of the decimal point using the "9" selector.

- Specifies one digit to the right of the decimal point.

- Includes a "%" after digit selectors.

```
proc tabulate data=bbu.scores noseps;
   class score;
   format score score.;
   table (score all)
         ,
         (N='Frequency'*f=comma10.
          pctn='ROW %'*f=pct.
         )/rts=10 misstext=' ';
run;
```

The format **score** is assigned with the FORMAT statement.

Picture pct is assigned using the f= format option for the PCTN.

Figure 4.3

	Frequency	ROW %
score LT 200	6,022	60.2%
GT 200	3,978	39.7%
All	10,000	100.0%

Output 4.1

4.4 Using the ROUND Option

If you examine the output in Section 4.3, you will notice that the second percentage statistic should be rounded up to 39.8%. The first time I saw this I was ready to give up on **Picture** formats. However, upon further reading of SAS Help and Documentation I learned that **Picture** formats truncate trailing digits by default. In order to round results, you need to specify the ROUND option for the **Picture FMTNAME**. The ROUND option will not always handle rounding as in the example where there are three groups, each with a 1/3 of the total frequency.

To round results, change the PICTURE statement to look like this:

```
Picture pct (round) low-high = '009.9%'
;
```

	Frequency	ROW %
score LT 200	6,022	60.2%
GT 200	3,978	39.8%
All	10,000	100.0%

Output 4.2

This is just one of the many "gotchas" that you have to watch out for. The default for INVALUE and VALUE statements is round; the default for the PICTURE statement is truncate.

4.5 PREFIX Option: An Example Using Negative Values

With **Picture** formats, all text before the first digit selector is ignored. To add text before the first digit selector, use the PREFIX= LABEL option. The following PICTURE examples show how to add various prefix characters.

- Negative signs for percentages:
  ```
  picture pct (round) low - <0 = '009.99%' (prefix='-')
                      0 - high = '009.99%'
      ;
  ```
- Negative and dollar signs:
  ```
  picture dol (round) low - <0 = '000,009.99' (prefix='-$')
                      0 - high = '000,009.99' (prefix='$')
      ;
  ```

4.6 Specifying Label Widths for Picture Formats

Unlike SAS internal formats, when using a **Picture** format that does not have a wide enough label, the result will truncate leading digits, prefix values, or both. Using an internal SAS format, if the value does not fit the *w.d* specification, SAS will try to adjust to a **BESTw.d** format and issue the following error message:

```
NOTE: At least one W.D format was too small for the number to be printed. The
decimal may be shifted by the "BEST" format.
```

Using **Picture** formats will not provide the warning message in the SAS log nor will there be a switch to a **BESTw.d** format when outputting. It is therefore important to test your **Picture** formats and add enough leading zeros to deal with possible values that were not thought of initially when designing the **Picture** formats.

We can test our **Picture** formats with simple code that will generate example values with their formatted results. It is worthwhile to test your **Picture** formats to see if the results are what you expect. The following code shows the problem with a user-defined **Picture** format:

```
proc format;
  picture dol (round) low-<0  = '0,009' (prefix='-$')   ❶
                      0-high = '0,009' (prefix='$')
    ;
run;
```

```
data _null_;                                                        ❷
  do test = -50000, -1000, -10, -1.5, -0.5, .4, .5, 10, 1000,
50000,
            500000;                                                 ❸
    put test=  @20 'FORMATTED Result: ' test dol.;                  ❹
  end;
run;
```

The **dol Picture** format is defined in line ❶. You want to print out negative numbers with a prefix of '-$' and print out positive numbers with a prefix of '$'. The label also includes the comma as a thousands separator.

The format is tested using a _NULL_ DATA step starting in line ❷. After the DATA step runs, the _NULL_ DATA step processes data without creating a data set. It is useful when you are trying to conserve memory or disk space. It is used here for testing, but it is not required. The user-defined **Picture** format is tested within the DATA step with values generated from a DO loop in line ❸. For each value of TEST, output is sent to the SAS log listing the TEST value and the formatted value. (To send output to the Output window include a "FILE PRINT;" statement in your source code before the PUT statement.) The following output shows that only values between −100 and +100 were correctly printed. Note that very large values were only printed with a value of $0. It is best to check the results of the **Picture** format before releasing reports using the **Picture** format.

```
test=-50000       FORMATTED Result:   -$0
test=-1000        FORMATTED Result: 1,000
test=-10          FORMATTED Result:   -$10
test=-1.5         FORMATTED Result:   -$2
test=-0.5         FORMATTED Result:   -$1
test=0.4          FORMATTED Result:    $0
test=0.5          FORMATTED Result:    $1
test=10           FORMATTED Result:    $10
test=1000         FORMATTED Result: 1,000
test=50000        FORMATTED Result:    $0
test=500000       FORMATTED Result:    $0
```

Output 4.3

To remedy the problem, increase the number of leading zeros or leading blanks in the label. The prefix values also take up space that is allocated by the digit selectors ("0,0009"). Here is the new code and the resulting test:

```
proc format;
  picture dol (round) low-<0  = '000,000,009' (prefix='-$')
                      0-high = '000,000,009' (prefix='$')
  ;
run;

data _null_;
  do test = -50000, -1000, -10, -1.5, -0.5, .4, .5, 10, 1000, 50000,
            500000;
    put test=  @20 'FORMATTED Result: ' test dol.;
  end;
run;
```

```
test=-50000      FORMATTED Result:    -$50,000
test=-1000       FORMATTED Result:     -$1,000
test=-10         FORMATTED Result:        -$10
test=-1.5        FORMATTED Result:         -$2
test=-0.5        FORMATTED Result:         -$1
test=0.4         FORMATTED Result:          $0
test=0.5         FORMATTED Result:          $1
test=10          FORMATTED Result:         $10
test=1000        FORMATTED Result:      $1,000
test=50000       FORMATTED Result:     $50,000
test=500000      FORMATTED Result:    $500,000
```

Output 4.4

4.7 Controlling the Length of the Picture Format Label

You can add a length qualifier to the application of the **Picture** format much like the addition of the width specification used on internal SAS formats. For example, you can eliminate some of the blank spaces before the printing of the **Picture** format in the example shown in Section 4.6 by adding a width to the **FMTNAME** as follows:

```
put test=  @20 'FORMATTED Result: ' test dol8.;
```

```
test=-50000        FORMATTED Result: -$50,000
test=-1000         FORMATTED Result:  -$1,000
test=-10           FORMATTED Result:     -$10
test=-1.5          FORMATTED Result:      -$2
test=-0.5          FORMATTED Result:      -$1
test=0.4           FORMATTED Result:       $0
test=0.5           FORMATTED Result:       $1
test=10            FORMATTED Result:      $10
test=1000          FORMATTED Result:   $1,000
test=50000         FORMATTED Result:  $50,000
test=500000        FORMATTED Result: $500,000
```

Output 4.5

Adding a decimal value to the **Picture** format will not affect the output or change the number of significant decimal values displayed. Since the *w.d* qualifier is the same as *w.*, there is no need to add the *d* qualifier.

The same results are also possible using the DEFAULT FMTNAME option.

```
picture dol (round default=8) low-<0  = '000,000,009' (prefix='-$')
                              0-high = '000,000,009' (prefix='$')
;
```

4.8 Using Internal SAS Formats to Meet Your Needs

Check SAS internal formats to see whether a format already exists. Looking at the code that generated output displayed in Section 4.6, you see that the SAS **DOLLARw.d** format will provide the same functionality. You have to be aware of the length required in the *w.d* specification when using internal SAS formats. For the **DOLLARw.d** format, you need to include enough width (*w*) to account for the decimal points, digits, commas, negative signs, and dollar signs. Here is code that uses the internal format over the user-defined **Picture** format. Note that there is a difference in output since the "–" appears after the $ when using the **DOLLARw.d** format.

```
data _null_;
  do test = -50000, -1000, -10, -1.5, -0.5, .4, .5, 10, 1000,
50000,
             500000;
    put test=  @20 'FORMATTED Result: ' test dollar8.0;
  end;
run;
```

```
test=-50000          FORMATTED Result:  $-50,000
test=-1000           FORMATTED Result:   $-1,000
test=-10             FORMATTED Result:      $-10
test=-1.5            FORMATTED Result:       $-2
test=-0.5            FORMATTED Result:       $-1
test=0.4             FORMATTED Result:        $0
test=0.5             FORMATTED Result:        $1
test=10              FORMATTED Result:      $10
test=1000            FORMATTED Result:    $1,000
test=50000           FORMATTED Result:   $50,000
test=500000          FORMATTED Result:  $500,000
```

Output 4.6

4.9 The MULTIPLIER Option

The MULTIPLIER, or MULT for short, option in **Picture** formats is used to specify a multiplier factor that is applied to the value before the label is applied. The MULT option logic can seem counterintuitive. Let's try testing some **Picture** formats. The first test is to report currency in units of $1000. In the banking industry, this is sometimes reported as $M (not to be confused with $millions). Here are the code and output:

> This is the numeral "1," not the lowercase letter "L."

```
proc format;
   picture dolm (round) low-<0  = '000,000,009M'
                             (prefix='-$' mult=1e-3)  ❶
                  0-high = '000,000,009M'
                             (prefix='$'  mult=1e-3)  ❶
   ;
run;


data _null_;
   do test = -55678,  10, 1000, 51230, 500132;
     put test=  @20 'FORMATTED Result: ' test dolm.;
   end;
run;
```

```
test=-55678        FORMATTED Result:          -$56M
test=10            FORMATTED Result:            $0M
test=1000          FORMATTED Result:            $1M
test=51230         FORMATTED Result:           $51M
test=500132        FORMATTED Result:          $500M
```

Output 4.7

I used the 1e–3 for the MULT= specification in lines ❶ and ❷. The "1" is the numeral one and not the lowercase "L." I could have used 0.001 with the same results, however, I like to use scientific notation when using multipliers with a base of 10. 1En is equivalent to $1*10^n$. A positive value for n moves the decimal to the right n places. A negative n moves the decimal to the left n places. The PICTURE statement looks for the decimal point in the label. In this case we have no decimal point, so the multiplier multiplies values by 0.001. The next example looks at how multipliers handle embedded decimal points in the labels.

The following example shows results when a request is made for an extra digit to the right of the decimal point. We test the code by keeping the 1e–3 multiplier, but we add a digit to the right of the decimal point in the LABEL statement. Note that for the beginning user of **Picture** formats, the results are unexpected.

```
proc format;
   picture dolm (round) low-<0  = '000,000,009.9M'
                                   (prefix='-$' mult=1e-3)
                        0-high = '000,000,009.9M'
                                   (prefix='$'  mult=1e-3)
   ;
run;


data _null_;
   do test = -55678,  10, 1000, 51230, 500132;
     put test=  @20 'FORMATTED Result: ' test dolm.;
   end;
run;
```

```
test=-55678        FORMATTED Result:         -$5.6M
test=10            FORMATTED Result:          $0.0M
test=1000          FORMATTED Result:          $0.1M
test=51230         FORMATTED Result:          $5.1M
test=500132        FORMATTED Result:         $50.0M
```

Output 4.8

We multiplied by 1/1000 so we expected the same results as the previous run, but with an added digit to the right of the decimal point. However, remember that when we add a decimal point in the LABEL statement we really have two multipliers. There is one multiplier in the label (1e–1) that accounts for how many digits to the left of the last digit the decimal point is placed. The second multiplier is in the MULT option (1e–3). When we add the two multipliers, the overall effect is 1e–4. The result looks like each test value is multiplied by 1e–4 (or divided by 10,000). To print results to the nearest \$1000 with a significant digit to the right of the decimal, we have to decrease the MULT-specified option to 1e–2. With the scientific notation, we can add the values after the "e" to determine the final effect. Using 1e–2 in a MULT option, along with the implicit 1e–1 in the LABEL statement, the final result is to multiply the value by 1e–3 (or move the decimal point to the left three places).

The information in SAS Help and Documentation for the MULT= option is a bit different, but I find that taking into account the total multiplier effect (LABEL effect plus MULT effect) is a useful way to pick the correct MULT value. In SAS Help and Documentation, values are multiplied by the multiplier and the resulting digits are merged into the PICTURE statement with the decimal point placed accordingly—for example, evaluating a value of 1000 with PICTURE ABC 1000-9999='9999.99' (MULT=10):

1000 * 10 = 10000. Placing the decimal point two digits from the right results in the label of 0100.00.

Going back to the problem, we can modify the previous code to get the desired results:

```
proc format;
  picture dolm (round) low-<0  = '000,000,009.9M'                 ❶
                                (prefix='-$' mult=1e-2)           ❷
                     0-high = '000,000,009.9M'
                                (prefix='$'  mult=1e-2)
  ;
run;


data _null_;
  do test = -55678,  10, 1000, 51230, 500132;
    put test=  @20 'FORMATTED Result: ' test dolm.;
  end;
run;
```

```
test=-55678        FORMATTED Result:        -$55.7M
test=10            FORMATTED Result:          $0.0M
test=1000          FORMATTED Result:          $1.0M
test=51230         FORMATTED Result:         $51.2M
test=500132        FORMATTED Result:        $500.1M
```

Output 4.9

4.10 Additional Options to Use with the PICTURE Statement

The options that apply to VALUE statements apply to PICTURE statements as well. Here we review some of the additional options that you can use with the PICTURE statement.

Use the NOEDIT LABEL option when you want to use the label as is without any edits of the digits. Here is an example:

```
proc format;
   picture dolm (round) low-0   = '000,000,009.9M'
                                     (prefix='-$' mult=1e-2)
                    0-100000 = '000,000,009.9M'
                                     (prefix='$'  mult=1e-2)
               100000-high = 'GE $100,000' (noedit)
   ;
run;

data _null_;
   do  test = -55678,  10, 1000, 51230, 500132;
     put test=  @20 'FORMATTED Result: ' test dolm.;
   end;
run;
```

```
test=-55678        FORMATTED Result:        -$55.7M
test=10            FORMATTED Result:          $0.0M
test=1000          FORMATTED Result:          $1.0M
test=51230         FORMATTED Result:         $51.2M
test=500132        FORMATTED Result:     GE $100,000
```

Output 4.10

With SAS 8 and later, there are a number of date/time directives that can be used with **Picture** formats. More information is available in SAS Help and Documentation. Here is an example to get you started. The example can be used to output the date and time generated.

```
proc format;
  picture dt
   low-high = 'TIME STAMP: %A %B %d, %Y.'
               (datatype=date)
  ;
  picture tm
    low-high = '%I:%M.%S%p'
               (datatype=time);

data _null_;
  file print;
  now = today();
  tm = time();
  put   now dt40.  tm tm.;
run;
```

Date/Time Directive Used in Code:

- %A: Full weekday name.
- %B: Full month name.
- %d: Day of month as decimal without leading zeros.
- %Y: Year with century as decimals.
- %I: Hour (12-hour clock) as decimal with no leading zeros.
- %M: Minute as decimal with no leading zeros.
- %S: Second as decimal without leading zeros.
- %p: A.M. or P.M.

Figure 4.4

Here is the output:

```
TIME STAMP: Sunday February 15, 2004. 7:22.51PM
```

The DATATYPE option tells SAS that the type of data value is DATE, TIME, or DATETIME. Note that I called the format using dt40. to extend the width of the label to 40 bytes since the width of the label defined in the PICTURE statement was only 25 bytes long and would have truncated the output of the date.

More Information

More information about the PICTURE statement can be found in SAS Help and Documentation.

CHAPTER 5

DATA Step Applications

5.1 Chapter Overview **66**

5.2 Table Lookup Variable Assignment **66**

5.3 Two-Dimensional Table Lookup **68**

5.4 Using PUTC and PUTN with Macro Variables **70**

5.5 Using PROC FORMAT to Extract Data **72**

5.6 Using PROC FORMAT for Data Merges: Creating Formats from Data **72**

5.7 Applying DATA Step Formats to Outlier Trimming **75**

5.1   Chapter Overview

Most of the examples we've looked at so far use PROC FORMAT to format data for output in reports. We can also use the table lookup functionality of PROC FORMAT in DATA step applications. In this chapter we will look at a number of applications where PROC FORMAT comes in handy in the DATA step.

Section 5.2 specifies how to assign new variables using user-defined formats or informats. The values of one variable are used to create the values of a new variable.

Section 5.3 shows how to extend the table lookup to a two-dimensional problem. We introduce the PUTC and PUTN functions to assign formats to use when evaluating the table lookup.

In Section 5.4, using %SYSFUNC and the PUTC or PUTN functions, we can assign labels to variables called by macro variables.

In Section 5.5, we see an application for subsetting data with user-defined formats.

In Section 5.6, we look at using user-defined formats or informats to run data merges against large unsorted data sets. In this section, we introduce how to create formats directly from special Cntlin data sets. This is a useful feature when we have many values to set up.

Section 5.7 shows how to set up more than one user-defined format from a single pass of the Cntlin data set. We show an application for outlier trimming.

5.2   Table Lookup Variable Assignment

We can use the table lookup feature of PROC FORMAT to assign values to new variables based on the values of an existing variable. You can use PROC FORMAT to replace IF-THEN/ELSE logic in your code.

The first example maps a credit line assignment to observations in the Scores data set based on their credit score values. For the simulated data, assume that higher scores predict lower risk, so we want to assign higher credit lines to applicants who have higher scores. Credit line assignment in practice is more complicated, but for this example, assume that the user wants to map credit line as a function of Score. The code shows how to assign the credit line using a user-defined informat. We then see how to make the assignment using a user-defined format. Here are the two sets of code:

Table Lookup Using a User-Defined Informat

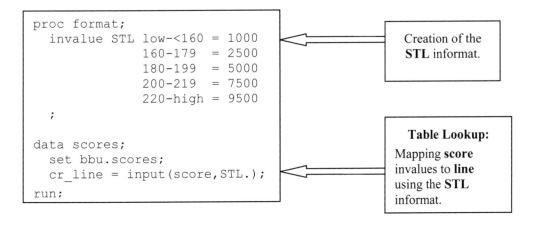

```
proc format;
   invalue STL low-<160 = 1000
               160-179 = 2500
               180-199 = 5000
               200-219 = 7500
               220-high = 9500
   ;

data scores;
   set bbu.scores;
   cr_line = input(score,STL.);
run;
```

Creation of the **STL** informat.

Table Lookup:
Mapping **score** invalues to **line** using the **STL** informat.

Figure 5.1

Table Lookup Using a User-Defined Format

```
proc format;
   value STL low-<160 = 1000
             160-179 = 2500
             180-199 = 5000
             200-219 = 7500
             220-high = 9500
   ;

data scores;
   set bbu.scores;
   cr_line =
input(put(score,STL.),best12.);
```

Creation of the **STL** format.

Table Lookup:
Mapping **score** invalues to **line** using the **STL** format and the **BEST12** informat.

Figure 5.2

Both methods generate the new Scores data set that has a new variable called Line. The Line variable is generated from a table lookup that was specified in PROC FORMAT. In each of the previous examples, Score groups map to the numeric Line variable.

Using the informat example, we get a warning message that numeric values had been converted to character values in the INPUT function. The format example did not generate such a warning. To avoid warning messages in the log, you can opt for the example using the format creation.

5.3   Two-Dimensional Table Lookup

You can use PROC FORMAT to generate a value based on values of two other variables. In this example, the assignment of the Line variable depends on the Score and Income_Est variables. We want to assign the Line variable based on the following assignment-specification table:

		INCOME Estimate:			
		low-<35,000	35,000-<45,000	45,000-<55,000	55,000+
	low-<160	500	750	1000	1250
	160-179	1500	2000	2500	3000
SCORE	180-199	4000	4500	5000	6000
	200-219	7000	7500	8000	8500
	220-high	9000	10000	15000	20000

Table 5.1

Code to generate the two-dimensional table lookup is shown here:

```
proc format;
  value score_f low-<160 = 'INCA'                              ❶
                160-179  = 'INCB'
                180-199  = 'INCC'
                200-219  = 'INCD'
                220-high = 'INCE'
  ;
  value INCA low-<35000=' 500' 35000-<45000='750' 45000-<55000='1000'
             55000-high='1250'
  ;
  value INCB low-<35000='1500' 35000-<45000='2000' 45000-<55000='2500'
             55000-high='3000'
  ;
  value INCC low-<35000='4000' 35000-<45000='4500' 45000-<55000='5000'
             55000-high='6000'
  ;
  value INCD low-<35000='7000' 35000-<45000='7500' 45000-<55000='8000'
             55000-high='8500'
  ;
  value INCE low-<35000='9000' 35000-<45000='10000' 45000-<55000='15000'
             55000-high='20000'
  ;

data scores;
  set bbu.scores;
  fmtuse = put(score,score_f.);                                ❷
  line = input(putn(income_est,fmtuse),best12.);               ❸
run;
```

The VALUE statement in line ❶ maps the Score variable to a label that will identify the specific format to use when evaluating the Income_Est variable. We then define five formats that will map credit line as a function of Income_Est.

The DATA step applies the user-defined formats. In line ❷ we create the character variable Fmtuse using the PUT function. Fmtuse maps SCORE groupings to five labels defined by the **SCORE_F** format (INCA, INCB, INCC, INCD, INCE). Line ❸ maps the Income_Est variable to the Line variable using the format named by the Fmtuse variable. Note that we use the PUTN function since the Income_Est variable is numeric. We would use the PUTC function if the variable we were applying to the format were character. Also note that there is no period after the Fmtuse variable, which contains the name of the format to use in the PUTN function. The INPUT function in line ❸ is used to convert the character variable to numeric. PUT functions (PUT, PUTN, and PUTC) always return character variables.

The reader is left to verify that the line assigment was performed correctly.

5.4 Using PUTC and PUTN with Macro Variables

You can apply user-defined formats to macro variables by using the special macro functions %SYSFUNC and PUTC or PUTN. An example is shown below.

In this example we want to apply labels to variables in a data set in which we did not include LABEL statements. We then want to run PROC UNIVARIATE on these variables with labels determined from a format.

Code and output are listed here:

```
libname bbu 'C:\BBU FORMAT\DATA';

proc format;
   value $var   'age'     = 'Age of Responder'
                'agediag' = 'Age Diagnosed'
                'dosage'  = 'Daily Dosage'
   ;
   picture dosage (round)low-high = '0009.99mg'
   ;
run;

%macro histo(var);
 proc univariate data=bbu.Aghd;
   var &var;
   label &var="%sysfunc(putc(&var,$var.))";
   format dosage dosage.;
   histogram &var  /     vscale     = count
                         cframe     = ligr
                         cfill      = gwh
                         pfill      = solid
                         legend     = legend1;
   inset n mean  median min max /header='Summary Statistics'
                         cfill  = white
                         ctext  = black;
   legend1 cframe=gray cborder=black;
   title;
   run;
%mend;

%histo(age)
```

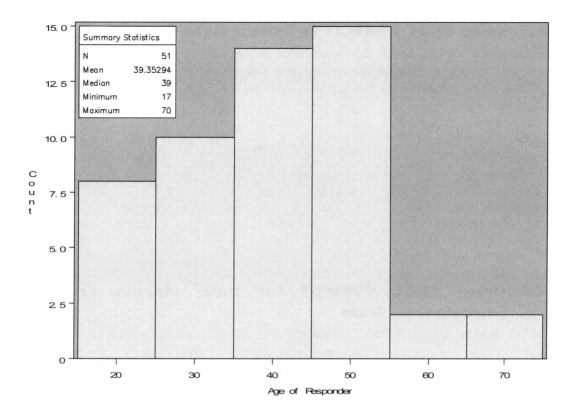

Output 5.1

5.5 Using PROC FORMAT to Extract Data

PROC FORMAT can be used to subset data when generating new data. This example extracts records from a larger data set when a key field matches certain values. Line ❶ applies the format to a Key variable. If the PUT function returns an "NG" the record is not included in the subset data.

```
proc format;
   value $key '06980', '0698F', '0699H' = 'OK'
              other                      = 'NG'
   ;

data stuff;
   set large.stuff;
   if put(key,$key.)= 'NG' then delete;                    ❶
run;
```

5.6 Using PROC FORMAT for Data Merges: Creating Formats from Data

The first time I used PROC FORMAT to match files was when a colleague came to me one day asking for help in extracting records from large credit card transaction files. She had about 10,000 unique account numbers that she wanted to match against large transaction files that were not sorted by account number. My colleague did not want to sort the large number of mainframe tapes (over 100) by account number and she wanted an alternative to the sort and merge approach. The solution was to let PROC FORMAT build a table lookup and then apply the format when reading the transaction files. The solution is outlined in this section.

The first step is to create a special data set of the 10,000 records that would be used to build the format. The data set must have unique keys (account numbers) and must have a few special variables:

- Fmtname: The name of the format to create.

- Type: "C" for a character format, "N" for a numeric format, "I" for a numeric informat, "J" for a character informat, and "P" for a **Picture** format.

- Start: The value. If there is a range to specify, you will also need the End variable.

- Label: The label to apply to the range.

The smaller data set must be sorted by a key field (Accn) and duplicates should be eliminated. For the example code, the smaller data set, Small, represents the 10,000 unique account numbers. The transaction file is called Test. The unique key to match (or extract) on is called Accn. The code is as follows:

```
proc sort data=small (keep=accn) nodupkey force;          ❶
  by accn;
run;

data fmt (rename=(accn=start));                           ❷
  retain fmtname 'key'                                    ❸
         type 'N'
         label 'Y';
  set small;

proc format cntlin=fmt;                                   ❹
run;

data matched;
  set test;
  where put(accn,key.)='Y';                               ❺
run;
```

The Small data set must be sorted (❶) with the NODUPKEY option to ensure that ranges are not duplicated. The FORCE option replaces the data set and destroys any indexes. This option is not required. For duplicate key records, the NODUPKEY option retains the first record and eliminates subsequent duplicate records.

The Fmt data set contains specific variables to create the format. The Accn variable is the match key and is renamed with the required variable Start (❷). The other required variables, Fmtname, Type, and Label are generated with the RETAIN statement (❸). Note that we could have also saved the Fmt data set as a SAS view:

```
data fmt (rename=(accn=start))/view=fmt;
```

This will save disk space.

The Key format is created with the CNTLIN option in line ❹. The format is applied in the subsequent DATA step in line ❺. Any account ID that matches one of the 10,000 unique records in the Small data set will return a formatted label of "Y" and will be outputted to the Matched data set.

Any record that does not match Accn will not be formatted to a "Y." The result of the PUT function will be the first byte of the Accn variable. Since the WHERE condition is not satisfied for nonmatched records, nonmatched records are not outputted to the data set Matched. The goal is to extract only those records that will return a "Y" in the application of the format.

Note that when I ran PROC FORMAT to match records, I got the following error message:

```
ERROR: PUT function reported 'ERROR: Invalid value for width
specified - width out of range' while processing WHERE clause.
```

If you want to run the code without the error message, you can specify a specific formatted label for all account numbers that do not match. This is done by specifying an OTHER condition in the Fmt data set. The code is shown here:

```
data fmt (rename=(accn=start));
   retain fmtname 'key'
          type 'N'
          label 'Y';
   set small end=eof;
   output;
   if eof then do;
     HLO='O';                                               ❶
     label='N';
     output;
   end;
```

Line ❶ sets up the OTHER condition with the HLO variable that is reserved for HIGH, LOW, and OTHER specifications.

In my original application of match-merging data, I used this technique to process a flat file and to output the entire record for any matched records. This can be done by modifying the previous DATA step as follows:

```
data _null_;
   infile test missover;
   file extract;
   input @1 accn 6.;
   if put(accn,key.)='Y' then put _infile_;
run;
```

On z/OS operating systems, you will need JCL code to identify files referenced by the Infile and File lines.

This method depends on the amount of memory available to store the format. It can work for up to 100,000 records using a format to match against many millions of unsorted records. The procedure is efficient because there is no need to sort the larger file that we want to match against.

You can also set up the Cntlin data set using SQL. For an example see Perry Watts's paper titled "Using Format Concatenation in SAS Software to Decode Data in Longitudinal Studies."

5.7 Applying DATA Step Formats to Outlier Trimming

An application to identify outliers or to trim outlier values was suggested by Jack Shoemaker at NESUG 1998. Using some modifications, here is an example of the technique. The application trims selected numeric variables at the 95th percentile. If a variable exceeds its 95th percentile, replace the value with the 95th percentile. Code is provided here. With this code, we show how to program the end of the range of values with the introduction of the End variable. The End variable is used to identify the ending value of a value or invalue range. When setting up a range of values, the Start variable identifies the start of the range and the End variable identifies the end of the range.

```
options nocenter errors=2 mprint;
libname bbu "C:\SAS BBU Format\DATA";

proc format;
  value sat 5     = 1                              ❶
            other = 0
  ;
```

```
%let vars = age agediag agestart dosage;                          ❷

proc means data=bbu.aghd noprint;                                 ❸
   var &vars;
   output out=trim p95=;
run;


%macro fmtcreate(var);                                            ❹
   fmtname = '_' || "&var" || '_';
   start = &var;
   end   = 'high';
   label = &var;
   output;
%mend;

data cntlin (keep=fmtname type  start end label);
   retain type 'N';
   length fmtname $10;                                            ❺
   set trim (keep=&vars);
   %fmtcreate(age)
   %fmtcreate(agediag)
   %fmtcreate(agestart)
   %fmtcreate(dosage)
run;

proc sort data=cntlin;
   by fmtname;
run;
proc format cntlin=cntlin fmtlib;                                 ❻
run;

%macro missing_trim(var);
   length fmtuse $10;
   fmtuse = '_' || "&var" || '_';
   &var = input(putn(&var,fmtuse),best.) <> 0;                    ❼
%mend;
```

```
data aghd_model;
  set book.aghd;
  /* dependent variable for logistic regression */
  sat=input(put(sat,sat.),1.);                              ❽
  /* set missing values to 0  and trim*/
  %missing_trim(age)
  %missing_trim(agediag)
  %missing_trim(agestart)
  %missing_trim(dosage)
run;

proc logistic data=aghd_model descending;                  ❾
  class sex;
  model sat = sex | age | agestart | dosage@2
              age*age agestart*agestart dosage*dosage
              /selection=stepwise sle=.05 sls=.05;
run;
```

Comments about the code:

- Line ❶ sets up a format to convert a Likert scale variable (Sat) with five levels into a binary variable.

- Line ❷ sets up variables that are to be trimmed at the 95th percentile. If a value exceeds the 95th percentile, set the value to the 95th percentile.

- Line ❸ generated an output data set with 95th percentile values for variables that are specified in the macro variable &vars.

- Line ❹ sets up a macro to apply in creating the Format data set. Note that **FMTNAME** is padded with leading and trailing dashes. This is done to prevent variables with leading or trailing numbers from being specified in format names. I have specified the End variable as "high," which could have been done with an HLO variable as well. The format ranges are from the 95th percentile to high with a resulting label set to the 95th percentile.

The macro variable fmtcreate gets called in creating the data set Cntlin. The macro variable generates the required data elements for the Cntlin data set. Here is the log output for the macro call:

```
59    data cntlin (keep=fmtname type  start end label);
60       retain type 'N';
61       length fmtname $10;
62       set trim (keep=&vars);
63       %fmtcreate(age)
MPRINT(FMTCREATE):    fmtname = '_' || "age" || '_';
MPRINT(FMTCREATE):    start = age;
MPRINT(FMTCREATE):    end = 'high';
MPRINT(FMTCREATE):    label = age;
MPRINT(FMTCREATE):    output;
64       %fmtcreate(agediag)
MPRINT(FMTCREATE):    fmtname = '_' || "agediag" || '_';
MPRINT(FMTCREATE):    start = agediag;
MPRINT(FMTCREATE):    end = 'high';
MPRINT(FMTCREATE):    label = agediag;
MPRINT(FMTCREATE):    output;
65       %fmtcreate(agestart)
MPRINT(FMTCREATE):    fmtname = '_' || "agestart" || '_';
MPRINT(FMTCREATE):    start = agestart;
MPRINT(FMTCREATE):    end = 'high';
MPRINT(FMTCREATE):    label = agestart;
MPRINT(FMTCREATE):    output;
66       %fmtcreate(Dosage)
MPRINT(FMTCREATE):    fmtname = '_' || "Dosage" || '_';
MPRINT(FMTCREATE):    start = Dosage;
MPRINT(FMTCREATE):    end = 'high';
MPRINT(FMTCREATE):    label = Dosage;
MPRINT(FMTCREATE):    output;
67    run;
```

Output 5.2

- **FMTNAME** must have a specified length (❺) when generating the Cntlin data set.

- Line ❻ sets up the formats from the Cntlin data set. The FMTLIB option is used to display information about each format. Output for only one of the formats is shown here:

```
                    FORMAT NAME: _AGEDIAG_ LENGTH: 2
  MIN LENGTH:   1  MAX LENGTH:  40  DEFAULT LENGTH   2  FUZZ: STD


START           END              LABEL   (VER. 9.1      11NOV2003:12:45:16)
52              HIGH             52
```

Output 5.3

- Line ❼ has two functions. The first uses the format to trim the variable to the 95th percentile, and second, the <> operator is a MAX operator that sets missing values and negative values to 0. We use the PUTN function since we created a user-defined format as opposed to an informat. The INPUT function converts the value from character to numeric. Also note that the informat used for the INPUT function did not contain a width or decimal specification. The results worked and SAS chose the default width of 12. Note that for any values that are less than the 95th percentile, the original value is returned.

- In line ❽ we set up Sat as a binary variable using the **SAT** format. We cannot do this in a procedure using either a FORMAT or INFORMAT statement. Formats will apply only to Class variables in procedures or variables in a TABLE statement in PROC FREQ.

- Line ❾ is the syntax for the PROC LOGISTIC step. Results are not shown.

More Information

More information about PROC FORMAT can be found in SAS Help and Documentation.

Shoemaker, J. 1998. "Advanced Techniques to Build and Manage User-Defined SAS FORMAT Catalogs." *Proceedings of the Eleventh Annual NorthEast SAS Users Group Conference*, Pittsburgh, PA, 102-107.

Watts, P. 1999. "Using Format Concatenation in SAS Software to Decode Data in Longitudinal Studies." *Proceedings of the Twelfth Annual NorthEast SAS Users Group Conference*, Washington, DC, 680-688.

CHAPTER 6

MULTILABEL Option: When One-to-One or Many-to-One Is Not Enough

6.1 Chapter Overview **82**

6.2 MULTILABEL Example **83**

6.1 Chapter Overview

In this chapter we will look at the MULTILABEL option that was introduced in PROC FORMAT in SAS 8. This option allows values to have overlapping or multiple labels. Application of the **Multilabel** format can be used in the TABULATE, MEANS, and SUMMARY procedures. We will look at an example using PROC TABULATE and PROC MEANS.

By default, PROC FORMAT will not allow you to create one-to-many or many-to-many values to labels. The default prevents unintentional mapping errors which are common with IF-THEN/ELSE code. An example of setting up a many-to-many format mapping is shown here:

```
13    proc format;

14      value scr low - 200   = 1

15              190 - 210   = 2

16              200 - high  = 0

17      ;

ERROR: These two ranges overlap: LOW-200 and 190-210 (fuzz=1E-12).

NOTE: The previous statement has been deleted.
```

Output 6.1

You can use the MULTILABEL option to intentionally create a one-to-many or a many-to-many table lookup. This chapter will show you how to create these special formats.

6.2 MULTILABEL Example

This example comes from hypothetical credit card application processing. There are three "Approval" decision codes and two "Decline" codes:

Decision Code Value	Label
a1	Approval
a2	Weak Approval
a4	Approved for Alternate Product
d1	Decline for Credit
d6	Decline for Other Reasons

Table 6.1

The task is to get frequency counts for each decision code and to get totals for approvals and declines. The following code generates hypothetical data and the formats used in the example:

```
proc format;
  value key low -     0.20 = 'a1'          ❶
             0.20 < - 0.25 = 'a2'
             0.25 < - 0.35 = 'a4'
             0.35 < - 0.80 = 'd1'
             0.80 < - high = 'd6'
  ;
  picture p8r (round)                       ❷
    low - < 0 = '0009.99%' (prefix='-')
    0 - high  = '0009.99%'
  ;
value $deccode (multilabel notsorted)       ❸
        'a1'        = 'a1: Approval'
        'a2'        = 'a2: Weak Approval'
        'a4'        = 'a4: Approved Alternate Product'
        'a0' - 'a9' = 'APPROVE TOTALS'
        'd1'        = 'd1: Decline for Credit'
        'd6'        = 'd6: Decline Other'
        'd0' - 'd9' = 'DECLINE TOTALS'
  ;
```

```
data decision;
  do id = 1 to 1000;
    decision = put(ranuni(7),key.);      ❹
    output;
  end;
```

In the PROC FORMAT section of the code we create three formats:

- In line ❶ we generate the format that will assign decision codes to records in a SAS data set based on a uniform random number that is generated in a DO loop in line ❹.

- The second format in line ❷ generates the **Picture** format for displaying percent signs in PROC TABULATE.

- The final format in line ❸ is used to generate the **Multilabel** format. The NOTSORTED option was used so that the labels would not sort in reports.

Some comments about the **Multilabel** format created in line ❸:

- Note that we must specify the MULTILABEL option when generating the format.

- Note that there are labels for each of the five decision codes. We also map all codes beginning with the letter "a" to "APPROVE TOTALS" and all those beginning with the letter "d" to "DECLINE TOTALS."

We can now generate frequency counts using PROC MEANS (or PROC SUMMARY). The CLASS statement specifies the Decision variable with the MLF option, which indicates that it will be formatted using a **Multilabel** format. Include the PRELOADFMT option with order=data to display the labels in the order specified in PROC FORMAT. Output is shown after the code.

```
proc means data=decision n;
  class decision/mlf preloadfmt order=data;
  format decision $deccode.;
run;
```

```
The MEANS Procedure

          Analysis Variable : id


                                          N
   decision                              Obs          N

   ─────────────────────────────────────────────

   a1: Approval                          163         163


   a2: Weak Approval                      45          45


   a4: Approved Alternate Product        106         106


   APPROVE TOTALS                        314         314


   d1: Decline for Credit                453         453


   d6: Decline Other                     233         233


   DECLINE TOTALS                        686         686

   ─────────────────────────────────────────────
```

Output 6.2

We can also generate a report using PROC TABULATE. Here are the code and output:

```
proc tabulate data=decision
              noseps
              formchar='                 ';
   class decision/mlf preloadfmt order=data;
   format decision $deccode.;
   table (decision all)
         ,n*f=comma5.
       pctn='%'*f=p8r.
       /rts=33 row=float misstext=' ';
   run;
```

	N	%
Decision		
a1: Approval	163	16.30%
a2: Weak Approval	45	4.50%
a4: Approved Alternate Product	106	10.60%
APPROVE TOTALS	314	31.40%
d1: Decline for Credit	453	45.30%
d6: Decline Other	233	23.30%
DECLINE TOTALS	686	68.60%
All	1,000	100.00%

Output 6.3

More information about using PROC TABULATE can be found in SAS Help and Documentation or in a NESUG paper I presented in 2001 titled "Making Sense of PROC TABULATE."

Also note that if you build a **Multilabel** format using a Ctlin data set you must include an HLO variable set to a value of "M."

More Information

More information about PROC FORMAT and PROC TABULATE can be found in SAS Help and Documentation.

Bilenas, J. 2001. "Making Sense of PROC TABULATE." *Proceedings of the Fourteenth Annual NorthEast SAS Users Group Conference*, Baltimore, MD, 201-205.

Bilenas, J. 2005. "Making Sense of PROC TABULATE." *Proceedings of the Thirtieth Annual SAS Users Group International Conference*, Philadelphia, PA, 243-30.

CHAPTER 7

Managing Format Catalogs

7.1 Chapter Overview.. **90**

7.2 Storing Formats... **90**

7.3 Viewing Stored Formats **92**

7.4 Viewing and Modifying the Format Catalog **94**

7.5 Transporting Stored Formats **96**

7.1   Chapter Overview

When we create a user-defined format, the resulting format will be stored in a temporary SAS catalog named FORMATS. In this chapter we will review how to create and manage permanent format catalogs.

We will first review how to save a user-defined format or informat. The discussion will focus on creating permanent format catalogs and how to use these stored formats in future applications.

7.2   Storing Formats

There are occasions when you want to permanently store a format or informat. Reasons for doing so are as follows:

- If the format or informat is large, storing the catalog will make each easier to manage.

- Stored formats and informats do not have to be respecified in the source code.

- You can share the stored catalogs of formats or informats with colleagues by letting them know the location of the catalog.

The simplest way to store a format or informat catalog is to store it under a LIBNAME named LIBRARY. By default SAS looks for formats or informats in a temporary catalog called WORK, followed by LIBRARY, and then followed by other LIBNAMES specified by the FMTSEARCH option.

Let's take the **$SEX** format as an example and change the code so that the format is saved as a permanent catalog. The code is listed here:

```
libname library 'c:\temp';

proc format library=library;
   value $sex 'M' = Male
              'F' = Female
   ;
run;
```

To use the stored format again in other code, include the LIBRARY LIBNAME statement in your code. There is no need to regenerate the format with PROC FORMAT code.

The catalog is stored under the catalog named LIBRARY.FORMATS. If you look in the c:\temp directory when you run the above code, you will see a file named formats.sas7bcat. In this example, we stored only one format; however, you can add as many formats, informats, or **Picture** formats as you want and they will all be stored in the formats.sas7bcat file that is specified in the LIBRARY LIBNAME statement.

You can store the catalog in a LIBNAME specification other than LIBRARY, but then the LIBNAME statement must be specified in the FMTSEARCH option. For example, if you want to store the catalog under a LIBNAME called FMLIB, then apply the following OPTION statement:

    OPTIONS FMTSEARCH = (FMLIB);

As a final option, you do not have to store the format in a catalog with the name FORMATS. You can specify any second-level name. Here is an example:

```
proc format library=library.fmtest;
   value $sx 'M' = 'MALE'
             'F' = 'FEMALE'
             other = 'OTHER'
   ;
run;
```

However, when you want to use the **$SX** format stored in library.fmtest you will need to use the FMTSEARCH option as follows:

```
options nocenter fmtsearch=(work library.fmtest);
```

7.3 Viewing Stored Formats

We saw in Chapter 5 that the FMTLIB option can display catalog contents using PROC FORMAT. Application to the $SX code is shown here:

```
proc format library=library.fmtest fmtlib;
run;
```

```
          FORMAT NAME: $SX        LENGTH:    6    NUMBER OF VALUES:    3

    MIN LENGTH:   1   MAX LENGTH:   40   DEFAULT LENGTH    6   FUZZ:          0

  START               END               LABEL    (VER. V7|V8    15DEC2003:15:58:13)

  F                   F                 FEMALE

  M                   M                 MALE

  **OTHER**           **OTHER**         OTHER
```

Output 7.1

You can also get information about the format with the CNTLOUT option. An example is shown here:

```
proc format library=library.fmtest cntlout=test;
run;

proc contents data=test;
proc print noobs data=test;  var fmtname start end label;
run;
```

```
          Alphabetic List of Variables and Attributes


   #      Variable     Type     Len      Label


  20      DATATYPE     Char       8      Date/time/datetime?

  18      DECSEP       Char       1      Decimal separator

   7      DEFAULT      Num        3      Default length

  19      DIG3SEP      Char       1      Three-digit separator

  16      EEXCL        Char       1      End exclusion

   3      END          Char       9      Ending value for format

  12      FILL         Char       1      Fill character

   1      FMTNAME      Char      32      Format name

   9      FUZZ         Num        8      Fuzz value

  17      HLO          Char      11      Additional information

   4      LABEL        Char       6      Format value label

  21      LANGUAGE     Char       8      Language for date strings

   8      LENGTH       Num        3      Format length

   6      MAX          Num        3      Maximum length

   5      MIN          Num        3      Minimum length

  11      MULT         Num        8      Multiplier

  13      NOEDIT       Num        3      Is picture string noedit?

  10      PREFIX       Char       2      Prefix characters

  15      SEXCL        Char       1      Start exclusion

   2      START        Char       9      Starting value for format

  14      TYPE         Char       1      Type of format
```

Output 7.2: Variable Listing of PROC CONTENTS Output

FMTNAME	START	END	LABEL
SX	F	F	FEMALE
SX	M	M	MALE
SX	**OTHER**	**OTHER**	OTHER

Output 7.3: PROC PRINT Listing Output

Note that PROC CONTENTS lists many more fields than we specified when we set up a format. Many of the fields are set as default fields and do not have to be prespecified.

7.4 Viewing and Modifying the Format Catalog

You can use PROC CATALOG to view and edit descriptions of the catalog. Here is code that will generate information on the stored **$SX** format:

```
proc catalog c=library.fmtest;
  contents;
run;
```

```
                    Contents of Catalog LIBRARY.FMTEST


#   Name    Type          Create Date          Modified Date      Description
_____

1   SX      FORMATC    29DEC2003:12:48:34    29DEC2003:12:48:34
```

Output 7.4

For more descriptive information, use the STAT option of the CONTENTS statement. Use a linesize of at least 121 to print across without wrapping text. Here are the code and output:

```
options ls=137;
proc catalog c=library.fmtest;
  contents stat;
run;
```

```
                          Contents of Catalog LIBRARY.FMTEST




                                                             Last   Last
                                                Page  Block  Num of  Block  Block
# Name  Type          Create Date    Modified Date Description Size   Size  Blocks Bytes  Size  Pages

1 SX    FORMATC  29DEC2003:12:48:34  29DEC2003:12:48:34       4096   4096     1    214    255      1
```

Output 7.5

Note that the description heading is blank. To add a description, use the following PROC CATALOG code:

```
proc catalog c=library.fmtest;
  modify sx.formatc (description='Sex Code Format');
  contents;
run;
```

```
                    Contents of Catalog LIBRARY.FMTEST
#      Name       Type        Create Date        Modified Date     Description


1      SX        FORMATC  29DEC2003:12:48:34   29DEC2003:13:12:57   Sex Code Format
```

Output 7.6

Note that PROC CATALOG is a RUN group processing procedure. It runs until a QUIT or CANCEL statement is issued and submitted. It required only one PROC CATALOG statement to start PROC CATALOG.

There are other functions available to you in PROC CATALOG. You can also use PROC CATALOG to rename, delete, copy, or move formats. More information is available in SAS Help and Documentation.

7.5 Transporting Stored Formats

There are a number of options you have to transport the catalog from one destination to another. One possibility is to transfer the original code that was used to create the catalog.

If the source and destination use the same operating systems, you can copy and paste the catalog from one destination to the other. If the two systems run on different operating systems, you will need to create a transport copy of the catalog using PROC CPORT. After the file is copied to the destination site, use PROC CIMPORT to create the system-specific catalog on the system you are transporting the catalog to.

PROC MIGRATE is a new procedure introduced in SAS 9.1 that moves older SAS libraries directly to SAS 9.1. SAS provides a calculator to help with the migration of libraries using PROC MIGRATE:

http://support.sas.com/rnd/migration/planning/files/migratecalc/

More Information

For information about working with format catalogs, see SAS Help and Documentation.

Shoemaker, J. 2002. "PROC FORMAT in Action." *Proceedings of the Twenty-seventh Annual SAS Users Group International Conference*, Orlando, FL, 56-27.

Shoemaker, J. 2001. "Eight PROC FORMAT Gems." *Proceedings of the Twenty-sixth Annual SAS Users Group International Conference*, Long Beach, CA, 62-26.

Shoemaker, J. 2000. "Ten Things you Should Know about PROC FORMAT." *Proceedings of the Thirteenth Annual NorthEast SAS Users Group Conference*, Philadelphia, PA, 242-246.

Shoemaker, J. 1998. "Creating a Self-Documenting FORMAT Catalog." *Proceedings of the Eleventh Annual NorthEast SAS Users Group Conference*, Pittsburgh, PA, 345-346.

LaPann, K. 2004. "Handling SAS@ Formats Catalogs across Versions." *Proceedings of the Philadelphia Area SAS Users Group Conference*, Philadelphia, PA. Available via e-mail: Karin.lapann@astrazeneca.com

Index

SYMBOLS

$6. informat   3–4

A

Adult Growth Hormone Deficiency Survey data
      23–25
ATTRIB statement, assigning informats in DATA
      step   8–9

B

BESTw. format   14–17
binary search algorithm   22
blanks, leading   6, 32–34

C

CATALOG procedure, viewing and editing
      format catalogs   94–95
catalogs
      See format catalogs
character data, converting to numeric data   7,
      15–17
character informats   2
      internal   32–34
      specifying at run time   8
character variables, returning with PUT function
      13–14
$CHARw. format   11, 12
$CHARw. informat   3–4, 6, 32–34
CIMPORT procedure, transporting stored formats
      96

CNTLIN option, in data merge   74
CNTLOUT option, getting format information
      92
coded values, mapping into literals   20–21
column-delimited input 3–4
commas, embedded   4–6
COMMAw.d format   10
COMMAw.d informat   5–6, 10
CONTENTS procedure
      STAT option   94–95
      viewing stored formats   92–94
CPORT procedure, transporting stored
      formats   96
credit line assignment   66
currency, reporting in $1000 units   60–63

D

data, creating formats from   72–75
data merges   72–75
data sets
      in this book   22–26
      reading data into   3–4
DATA step, assigning informats in   8–9
DATA step applications   66–79
      data merges   72–75
      extracting data   72
      outlier trimming   75–79
      PUTC and PUTN with macro variables
            70–71
      table lookup variable assignment   66–68
      two-dimensional table lookup   68–69
DATATYPE option, with Picture formats   64
date/time directives, and Picture formats   64

date/time informats 2
decimals 4, 61–63
DEFAULT= option
    FUZZ option and 44
    INVALUE statement and 37
digit selectors 52–53
DO loops 84
dollar signs, embedded 4–6
DOLLAR*w.d* format 10, 59–60

E

efficiency 42
embedded commas and dollar signs 4–6
embedded formats and informats, within labels
        48–49
endpoint values 46
ERROR informat label 44
extracting data 72

F

FILE statement 12
flat files
    reading in data from 2
    writing out 11
FMTLIB option
    displaying format information 79
    viewing stored formats 92
FMTNAME 41–42
FMTSEARCH option, and storing formats 91
FORCE option, in data merges 73
format catalogs 90–96
    storing formats 90–91
    transporting stored formats 96
    viewing and modifying 94–95
    viewing stored formats 92–94
format names 30, 41–42
    length of 42
    name options 42–44
FORMAT procedure
    creating formats from data 72–75

data merges 72–75
    extracting data with 72
FORMAT statement 10
formats 9–17
    See also Picture formats
    See also stored formats
    See also user-defined formats
    BEST*w.* 14–17
    $CHAR*w.* 11, 12
    COMMA*w.d* 10
    creating from data 72–75
    DOLLAR*w.d* 10, 59–60
    embedded within labels 48–49
    function and usage 17
    information about 79, 92
    names 30, 41–44
    order of labels output 34–36
    specifying during run time 14
    storing 90–91
    vs. same-named informats 10
    Zw.d 13
FREQ procedure, ORDER=FORMATTED option
        35–36
frequency counts 84
FUZZ option 42–43, 44

H

hypothetical credit score data 25–26

I

IF-THEN statement, building table lookups
        21–22
IF-THEN/ELSE statement
    building table lookups 21–22
    VALUE statement and 30–32
INFMTNAME 41–42
INFORMAT statement 8–9
informats 2–9
    See also user-defined informats

$6. 3–4
assigning in DATA step 8–9
character informats 2, 8, 32–34
$CHAR*w.* 3–4, 6, 32–34
COMMA*w.d* 5–6, 10
date/time informats 2
embedded within labels 48–49
ERROR label 44
function and usage 17
LABEL_SAME_ 44
MMDDYY*w.* 3–4
numeric informats 2, 8
specifying at run time 8
vs. same-named formats 10
$*w.* 3–4, 32–34
w.d 3–4, 7
INPUT function 7
INPUT statement
    column-delimited 3–4
    reading data into variables 3–6
input values, mapping to output labels 20–22
INPUTC and INPUTN functions, specifying
        informats at run time 8
internal character informats, and user-defined
        formats 32–34
internal formats, instead of Picture formats
        59–60
INVALUE statement 28, 36–40
    DEFAULT=option and 37
    JUST option 38–40
    rules for using 40–48
    syntax 36
    UPCASE option 38–40
    user-defined informats 36–37

J

JUST option, INVALUE statement 38–40
justification
    left-justified invalues 38–40
    left-justified values 4, 12, 32–34
    right-justified values 6, 7, 12

L

labels
    applying to variables 70–71
    assigning 29–32
    default length of 44
    embedded formats and informats within
        48–49
    ERROR informat label 44
    mapping input values to output labels
        20–22
    maximum or minimum length of 44
    multiple or overlapping 82–87
    NOEDIT LABEL option 63
    order of output 34–36
    Picture formats and 52–53, 56–59, 63
    table lookup and 30–32
LABEL_SAME_ informat 44
leading blanks 6, 32–34
leading zeros 13
left-justified invalues 38–40
left-justified values 4, 12, 32–34
literals, mapping coded values into 20–21
LOGISTIC procedure, and outlier trimming
        79

M

macro variables, PUTC and PUTN functions
        with 70–71
many-to-many mapping 82–87
many-to-one mapping 20–22
mapping
    coded values into literals 20–21
    input values to output labels 20–22
    many-to-many 82–87
    many-to-one 20–22
    one-to-one 20–22
match-merging 72–75
MAX option 44
MEANS procedure, and MULTILABEL option
        84

merges 72–75
MIGRATE procedure, transporting stored
        formats 96
MIN option 44
missing values 46–48
MMDDYY*w.* informat 3–4
MULTILABEL option 82–87
MULTIPLIER option 60–63

N

negative values 56
nested formats and informats, within labels
        48–49
NODUPKEY option, and data merges 73
NOEDIT LABEL option 63
NOTSORTED option 42, 84
NULL keyword 11
numbers, templates for printing
        See Picture formats
numeric data
        converting character data to 7, 15–17
        outputting without format specification
                14–17
numeric informats 2
        specifying at run time 8

O

one-to-one mapping 20–22
ORDER=FORMATTED option, FREQ procedure
        35–36
outlier trimming 75–79
output, order of format labels 34–36
output labels, mapping input values to 20–22
outputting data
        See formats
overlapping labels 82–87

P

percentages, printing in TABULATE procedure
        53–55
Picture formats 52
        controlling label length 58–59
        DATATYPE option and 64
        date/time directives and 64
        digit selectors in label definitions
                52–53
        examples 53–55, 84
        internal formats instead of 59–60
        label widths 56–58
        MULTIPLIER option 60–63
        NOEDIT LABEL option 63
        PREFIX option 56
        printing percentages in TABULATE
                procedure 53–55
        ROUND option 55
        syntax 52
        testing 56–58
PICTURE statement 28
PREFIX option 56
PRELOADFMT option 84
PRINT procedure, FORMAT statement 10
printing numbers, templates for
        See Picture formats
printing percentages 53–55
PUT function 13–14
PUT statement 11–13
PUTC and PUTN functions 14
        macro variables with 70–71

R

reading data
        See informats
RETAIN statement, in data merges 73
right-justified values 6, 7, 12
ROUND option 55

rounding   16, 55
run-time specification   8, 14

S

SAS views   73
scientific notation   61–63
SET statement   11
$6. informat   3–4
STAT option, CONTENTS procedure   94–95
stored formats
    transporting   96
    viewing   92–94
storing formats   90–91
subsetting data   72
%SYSFUNC function   70–71

T

table lookup   20–22
    assigning labels and   30–32
    building with IF-THEN or IF-THEN/ELSE
        statements   21–22
    two-dimensional   68–69
    variable assignment with   66–68
TABULATE procedure
    MULTILABEL option and   86
    printing percentages in   53–55
templates for printing numbers
    See Picture formats
testing
    Picture formats   56–58
    user-defined formats and informats   43
transporting stored formats   96
two-dimensional table lookup   68–69

U

UNIVARIATE procedure   70–71
UPCASE option, INVALUE statement   38–40
uppercase invalues   38–40

user-defined formats
    See also format catalogs
    binary search algorithm for evaluating
        22
    internal character informats and   32–34
    length of names   42
    name options   42–44
    names   41–42
    specifying values   45–48
    testing   43
    VALUE statement and   30–32
user-defined informats
    binary search algorithm for evaluating
        22
    INVALUE statement and   36–37
    label specifications   44
    length of names   42
    name options   42–44
    names   41–42
    specifying invalues   45–48
    testing   43

V

VALUE keyword   30
VALUE statement   28
    IF-THEN/ELSE statement and   30–32
    rules for using   40–48
    user-defined formats and   30–32
variables
    applying labels to   70–71
    assigning with table lookup   66–68
    macro variables   70–71
    reading data into   3–6
    returning character variables   13–14

W

$w. informat   3–4, 32–34
w.d informat   3–4, 7

Y

YEARCUTOFF option, 4

Z

zeros, leading, 13
zip code data, 13
Zw.d format, 13

Books Available from SAS Press

Advanced Log-Linear Models Using SAS®
by **Daniel Zelterman** . . . . Order No. A57496

Analysis of Clinical Trials Using SAS®: A Practical
Guide
by **Alex Dmitrienko, Walter Offen,**
Christy Chuang-Stein,
and **Geert Molenbergs** . . . . Order No. A59390

Annotate: Simply the Basics
by **Art Carpenter** . . . . Order No. A57320

Applied Multivariate Statistics with SAS® Software,
Second Edition
by **Ravindra Khattree**
and **Dayanand N. Naik** . . . . Order No. A56903

Applied Statistics and the SAS® Programming
Language, Fourth Edition
by **Ronald P. Cody**
and **Jeffrey K. Smith** . . . . Order No. A55984

An Array of Challenges — Test Your SAS® Skills
by **Robert Virgile** . . . . Order No. A55625

Carpenter's Complete Guide to the SAS® Macro
Language, Second Edition
by **Art Carpenter** . . . . Order No. A59224

The Cartoon Guide to Statistics
by **Larry Gonick**
and **Woollcott Smith** . . . . Order No. A5515

Categorical Data Analysis Using the SAS® System,
Second Edition
by **Maura E. Stokes, Charles S. Davis,**
and **Gary G. Koch** . . . . Order No. A57998

Cody's Data Cleaning Techniques Using SAS® Software
by **Ron Cody** . . . . Order No. A57198

Common Statistical Methods for Clinical Research
with SAS® Examples, Second Edition
by **Glenn A. Walker** . . . . Order No. A58086

Debugging SAS® Programs: A Handbook of Tools
and Techniques
by **Michele M. Burlew** . . . . Order No. A57743

Efficiency: Improving the Performance of Your SAS®
Applications
by **Robert Virgile** . . . . Order No. A55960

The Essential PROC SQL Handbook for SAS® Users
by **Katherine Prairie** . . . . Order No. A58546

Fixed Effects Regression Methods for Longitudinal
Data Using SAS®
by **Paul D. Allison** . . . . Order No. A58348

Genetic Analysis of Complex Traits Using SAS®
Edited by **Arnold M. Saxton** . . . . Order No. A59454

A Handbook of Statistical Analyses Using SAS®,
Second Edition
by **B.S. Everitt**
and **G. Der** . . . . Order No. A58679

Health Care Data and the SAS® System
by **Marge Scerbo, Craig Dickstein,**
and **Alan Wilson** . . . . Order No. A57638

The How-To Book for SAS/GRAPH® Software
by **Thomas Miron** . . . . Order No. A55203

Instant ODS: Style Templates for the Output
Delivery System
by **Bernadette Johnson** . . . . Order No. A58824

In the Know... SAS® Tips and Techniques From Around
the Globe
by **Phil Mason** . . . . Order No. A55513

support.sas.com/pubs

*Integrating Results through Meta-Analytic Review Using
SAS® Software*
by **Morgan C. Wang**
and **Brad J. Bushman** . . . . Order No. A55810

The Little SAS® Book: A Primer, Second Edition
by **Lora D. Delwiche**
and **Susan J. Slaughter** . . . . Order No. A56649
(updated to include Version 7 features)

The Little SAS® Book: A Primer, Third Edition
by **Lora D. Delwiche**
and **Susan J. Slaughter** . . . . Order No. A59216
(updated to include SAS 9.1 features)

*Logistic Regression Using the SAS® System:
Theory and Application*
by **Paul D. Allison** . . . . Order No. A55770

Longitudinal Data and SAS®: A Programmer's Guide
by **Ron Cody** . . . . Order No. A58176

Maps Made Easy Using SAS®
by **Mike Zdeb**. . . . . Order No. A57495

*Multiple Comparisons and Multiple Tests Using
SAS® Text and Workbook Set*
(*books in this set also sold separately*)
by **Peter H. Westfall, Randall D. Tobias,
Dror Rom, Russell D. Wolfinger,**
and **Yosef Hochberg** . . . . Order No. A55770

Multiple-Plot Displays: Simplified with Macros
by **Perry Watts** . . . . Order No. A58314

*Multivariate Data Reduction and Discrimination with
SAS® Software*
by **Ravindra Khattree,**
and **Dayanand N. Naik** . . . . Order No. A56902

Output Delivery System: The Basics
by **Lauren E. Haworth** . . . . Order No. A58087

*Painless Windows: A Handbook for SAS® Users,
Third Edition*
by **Jodie Gilmore** . . . . Order No. A58783
(*updated to include Version 8 and SAS 9.1 features*)

PROC TABULATE by Example
by **Lauren E. Haworth** . . . . Order No. A56514

*Professional SAS Programmer's Pocket Reference,
Fifth Edition*
by **Rick Aster** . . . . Order No. A60075

Professional SAS® Programming Shortcuts
by **Rick Aster** . . . . Order No. A59353

Quick Results with SAS/GRAPH® Software
by **Arthur L. Carpenter**
and **Charles E. Shipp**. . . . . Order No. A55127

Quick Results with the Output Delivery System
by **Sunil Gupta** . . . . Order No. A58458

*Reading External Data Files Using SAS®: Examples
Handbook*
by **Michele M. Burlew** . . . . Order No. A58369

*Regression and ANOVA: An Integrated Approach
Using SAS® Software*
by **Keith E. Muller**
and **Bethel A. Fetterman** . . . . Order No. A57559

SAS® for Forecasting Time Series, Second Edition
by **John C. Brocklebank**
and **David A. Dickey** . . . . Order No. A57275

SAS® for Linear Models, Fourth Edition
by **Ramon C. Littell, Walter W. Stroup,**
and **Rudolf Freund** . . . . Order No. A56655

*SAS® for Monte Carlo Studies: A Guide for Quantitative
Researchers*
by **Xitao Fan, Ákos Felsovályi, Stephen A. Sivo,**
and **Sean C. Keenan** . . . . Order No. A57323

SAS® Functions by Example
by **Ron Cody** . . . . Order No. A59343

SAS® Macro Programming Made Easy
by **Michele M. Burlew** . . . . Order No. A56516

SAS® Programming by Example
by **Ron Cody**
and **Ray Pass** . . . . Order No. A55126

*SAS® Survival Analysis Techniques for Medical
Research, Second Edition*
by **Alan B. Cantor** . . . . Order No. A58416

support.sas.com/pubs

SAS® System for Elementary Statistical Analysis,
Second Edition
by **Sandra D. Schlotzhauer**
and **Ramon C. Littell**. . . . . Order No. A55172

SAS® System for Mixed Models
by **Ramon C. Littell, George A. Milliken, Walter W.**
Stroup, and **Russell D. Wolfinger** . . Order No. A55235

SAS® System for Regression, Second Edition
by **Rudolf J. Freund**
and **Ramon C. Littell**. . . . . Order No. A56141

SAS® System for Statistical Graphics, First Edition
by **Michael Friendly** . . . . Order No. A56143

The SAS® Workbook and Solutions Set
(*books in this set also sold separately*)
by **Ron Cody** . . . . Order No. A55594

Selecting Statistical Techniques for Social Science
Data: A Guide for SAS® Users
by **Frank M. Andrews, Laura Klem, Patrick M. O'Malley,**
Willard L. Rodgers, Kathleen B. Welch,
and **Terrence N. Davidson** . . . . Order No. A55854

Statistical Quality Control Using the SAS® System
by **Dennis W. King**. . . . . Order No. A55232

A Step-by-Step Approach to Using the SAS® System
for Factor Analysis and Structural Equation Modeling
by **Larry Hatcher**. . . . . Order No. A55129

A Step-by-Step Approach to Using the SAS® System
for Univariate and Multivariate Statistics,
Second Edition
by **Larry Hatcher, Norm O'Rourke,**
and **Edward J. Stepanski** . . . . Order No. A58929

Step-by-Step Basic Statistics Using SAS®: Student
Guide and Exercises
(*books in this set also sold separately*)
by **Larry Hatcher**. . . . . Order No. A57541

Survival Analysis Using the SAS® System:
A Practical Guide
by **Paul D. Allison** . . . . Order No. A55233

Tuning SAS® Applications in the OS/390 and z/OS
Environments, Second Edition
by **Michael A. Raithel** . . . . Order No. A58172

Univariate and Multivariate General Linear Models:
Theory and Applications Using SAS® Software
by **Neil H. Timm**
and **Tammy A. Mieczkowski**. . . . . . . Order No. A55809

Using SAS® in Financial Research
by **Ekkehart Boehmer, John Paul Broussard,**
and **Juha-Pekka Kallunki** . . . . Order No. A57601

Using the SAS® Windowing Environment:
A Quick Tutorial
by **Larry Hatcher**. . . . . Order No. A57201

Visualizing Categorical Data
by **Michael Friendly** . . . . Order No. A56571

Web Development with SAS® by Example
by **Frederick Pratter** . . . . Order No. A58694

Your Guide to Survey Research Using the
SAS® System
by **Archer Gravely**. . . . . Order No. A55688

JMP® Books

JMP® for Basic Univariate and Multivariate Statistics:
A Step-by-Step Guide
by **Ann Lehman, Norm O'Rourke, Larry Hatcher,**
and **Edward J. Stepanski** . . . . Order No. A59814

JMP® Start Statistics, Third Edition
by **John Sall, Ann Lehman,**
and **Lee Creighton** . . . . Order No. A58166

Regression Using JMP®
by **Rudolf J. Freund, Ramon C. Littell,**
and **Lee Creighton** . . . . Order No. A58789

support.sas.com/pubs

Titles in Art Carpenter's SAS® Software Series

Quick Results with the Output Delivery System
by Sunil K. Gupta
(Order No. A58458)

Annotate: Simply the Basics
by Art Carpenter
(Order No. A57320)

Multiple-Plot Displays: Simplified with Macros
by Perry Watts
(Order No. A58314)

Maps Made Easy Using SAS®
by Mike Zdeb
(Order No. A57495)

To order: support.sas.com/pubs
Or call: (800) 727-3228